A WALK

BETWEEN

HEAVEN AND EARTH

*A Personal Journal on Writing
and the Creative Process*

BURGHILD NINA HOLZER

Bell Tower • New York

Copyright © 1994 by Burghild Nina Holzer

All rights reserved. No part of this book may be
reproduced or transmitted in any form or by
any means, electronic or mechanical, including photocopying, recording,
or by any information storage and retrieval system,
without permission in writing from the publisher.

Published by Bell Tower, an imprint of Harmony Books,
a division of Crown Publishers, Inc., 201 East 50th Street,
New York, New York 10022.
Member of the Crown Publishing Group.

Random House, Inc. New York, Toronto, London, Sydney, Auckland

Bell Tower and colophon are trademarks of Crown Publishers, Inc.

Manufactured in the United States of America

Design by Debbie Glasserman

Library of Congress Cataloging-in-Publication Data
Holzer, B. Nina
A walk between heaven and earth: a personal journal on writing and the
creative process
B. Nina Holzer.—1st ed.
p.   cm.
1. Diaries—Authorship.   I. Title.
PN4390.H65   1994
818'.5403—dc20   93-32585
CIP

ISBN 0-517-88096-2

10 9 8 7 6 5 4 3 2 1

First Edition

A Walk Between
Heaven and Earth

For Sarah,

hope your own
path of writing
will be
beautiful,

B. M. Holzer

for my brother
who walked ahead
on the path

Starting Out

When one goes on a quest, one usually starts out with an intention. The intention might be some sort of goal—to find something, to have a vision, to arrive at a certain place. Or one might focus on the process, the path taken, paying attention to everything that happens on the way. Or, as in a walking meditation, one might focus on the walking itself— the movement, the breathing, the way one's foot meets the earth.

In writing this book, I combined all of these, as in fact many quests do. I had a goal of sorts. I wanted to produce a book for my students and wanted to document what I had been teaching in class, using the journal as a writing quest. But my particular interest for this journal was the path taken, the walk itself. Thus my strongest intention for this quest was to proceed in the form of a walking meditation—to take one step at a time, to let each journal entry come forth from the moment, to keep my focus on the subject of writing, and to record this.

A quest is a journey into the unknown. The writing process, any creative process, is also a journey into the unknown. A journal then is both the quest itself and a record of the quest. This is what makes it such an exciting adventure for me. It is also what makes the journal such a fine learning process. I trace my own steps on the page. And so, no matter what all my intentions were when I started out, this book is mostly a record of my own path, a writer's precarious journey through life.

In my own writing I had for years used the journal form as an experimental tool. My private journal was also a friend to me, an ear that could hear anything. But after years of random journal entries there were some unexpected insights into the nature of this process. I began to see that I was tracing something in the journal, that I was documenting something I was not conscious of.

I had come to realize that the writing process often produced altered states of consciousness in me that were very much like mystical visions. And I further came to see that without any conscious attempt, my journal had become a record of the sequence in which some mysterious process manifested itself in my writing and in my life.

As I gained more insight into this, I began to track myself more consistently in my journal, rereading it frequently, and I saw that a particular revelation in one entry had invariably triggered another in a later entry. I saw that certain themes had developed over weeks and months, and that random observations, thoughts, dreams, and sudden visionary images took place in a particular sequence. I began to trace these themes through my journal, and of course I could never tell how long it would take for the next piece in the sequence to show up. It might appear in the following entry, or it might be months down the road. Sometimes there were innumerable detours, but these often turned out to be subtle preparations for the next step.

The creative journey seemed to be very much like life—unpredictable, mysterious, full of sudden miracles, but yet with a very persistent structure to it. This structure did not live in my conscious will, but rather in some unconscious field of knowledge. As my own writing process continued, I began to trust that hidden field of knowledge. I knew I did not have to be in charge of it. In fact, the less I was in charge of it, the more miraculous it became.

The journal became a helpful tool to track my own journey, because on the one hand the journal is a linear form—the dated entries are chronological, so that in rereading it you can clearly see at what point in time a new image or insight emerged. But on the other hand the journal is not linear at all—you repeat yourself, you walk in a circle sometimes, finding yourself in the same place, reexamining the same issues from a different angle. And yet this form is perhaps neither linear nor circular. Entries are written in the moment—you do not make an outline for a journal, you write it as life is lived, you record in random fragments. And what you have in the end is a field with many points of entry, a live web with definite patterns. I grew to trust completely that these random journal entries over time would inevitably reveal the larger structures of my process.

As I applied this personal experience to my teaching of

writing, and to my work with people in general, I gradually understood that what we call the Creative Process is in no way limited to art or to individual acts of creating something. It is in fact a large ongoing movement in our lives, a force that has its own will and its own purpose, and which we manifest on many levels but in definite sequences. I saw that I was looking at a huge and, to me, profoundly sacred process, which was visible not just in my writing but in all aspects of my life and which the journal had involuntarily documented. It was from this point of my own insight that I began to write this book. For me, journal writing had become an exploration of my life process, in its continued metaphoric shape-shifting. I wanted this tool to be available to everyone, and I knew at this point that I was no longer just addressing students of creative writing but that this questing process on the page could be of value to people in many different situations.

This book was originally written six years ago. It documents a time span from the fall of 1987 to the summer of 1988. This may be helpful for the reader to know since some events in the book can be dated historically. However, this journal is essentially the record of a creative journey I took, thus perhaps timeless, and as relevant today as it was then. I have since rewritten it somewhat, but have been careful not to alter the actual journey that took place at the time.

It may also be important for the reader to know that this is not my private journal even though it contains many entries about my personal life. During the time of this writing quest I also kept a private journal. At the time I thought that mixing such a personal journal, which goes off into many different directions, with an ongoing focus on the process of writing would not work. Ironically, life broke into my focused writing meditation and could not be kept out. Thus my quest to document the writing process for my students also became the record of a truly personal passage.

B. Nina Holzer
Los Altos, California
Spring 1993

*A Walk Between
Heaven and Earth*

SAN FRANCISCO
NOVEMBER 6
FRIDAY, 5 P.M.

I began at the time of sunset.
Today I did not walk very far, only into my back
    room.
There I sat breathing in and out.
But when I opened my eyes,
there were two suns on the horizon
setting shoulder to shoulder,
so I wrote that into my journal.

5:30 P.M.

When you practice walking meditation, you go for a stroll.

—THICH NHAT HANH

The same is true for a journal. When you write in a journal, you go for a stroll, without purpose or direction, without a travel plan. You start now, and you walk for a while, write for a while, then you stop. What you have is a fragment. What you have is a record of your awareness. The next day you do it again. And perhaps the next day, and the next. What you have is many fragments—of yourself, of your mind, of your awareness of the world.

6 P.M.

I want to write a journal about journal writing. My students are always asking me to write down all that stuff that I teach them. But I don't want to write a textbook. I don't think that a textbook can really show the creative process. We learn by doing. I teach by doing. If I write textbook, I teach textbook. So I thought I would keep a journal instead. I thought I would take the risk and let my own writing process and my thoughts about writing unfold in this journal, and see what happens. Perhaps it would help people to trust their own writing quest.

I have kept journals for many years, and I have taught writing for a decade or more. My journal writing courses have gone under many names. When one teaches in an academic environment, as I often do, it is best to make up titles with much purpose and direction to them, as they are more likely to be approved for the curriculum that way. Thus I had "Journal Writing as a Source for Creative Writing," emphasizing its usefulness as a writer's notebook, "The Journal as a Literary Form," pointing to its legitimacy in the field of literature, "Writing a Personal Journal," hinting at its use in therapy and self-healing. In my private workshops, titles such as "A Writing Meditation," "A Vision Quest Journal," and "Writing the Green Mysteries" reflected the spiritual, shamanic, and environmental interests of our time. In the end it didn't matter what the title was, I was always teaching the same thing. I could have called it "The Expansion and Integration of Consciousness Through Writing," or I could have called it "Learning to Write in Curves." I am sure many more and wonderful titles come to mind, but the point is that we live at a time of great expansion of our conscious horizons and that the journal is a very flexible form of writing which can help in that process.

My own journal has been all of the above. I have kept notebooks that were a writer's experimental scratchbook, a woman's path of healing, a nature lover's field notes. I have done daily writing meditations, long spiritual quests on the page, and shamanic journeys into the world of visions and dreams. All of these were deep explorations into my own consciousness and into the nature of the world I am part of. But what stayed with me most consistently in all these writing journeys was that in each of them the journal involuntarily helped me to document my own creative process. It has become clear to me that this process itself is the most profound source of transformation in life. And for me, this creative path, whether in writing or in daily life, has become a mystical journey. I track my own footprints in the journal, and I teach writing in an attempt to help others walk this mysterious path of creation.

A student came to me one day, a fine older man. He was a retired engineer who had taken my class twice. He said, "Your journal writing class should really be called Creativity 1A." He said he wanted to write a book one day, that would help engineers understand the principles of the creative process. I didn't question him much, and assumed he meant that what he had learned in my writing class was applicable to other fields. I simply thanked him for the beautiful fragment he had read from his journal in class that day, pure poetry, pure meditation, written during a short walking exercise outdoors that required writing without any purpose whatsoever. The man died a year later, and the book for creative engineering never got written. But I know that it is the journal that changed his life during those last years. He died on a beautiful morning, returning from a walking/writing meditation, the notebook still in his hand, the last entry fresh on the page.

Which brings me back to Thich Nhat Hanh who wrote, "The purpose of walking meditation is walking meditation itself. Going is important, not arriving." The same is true for Creativity 1A. The same is true for journal writing. When you are in the flow of creation, you are here—going, walking, writing, but always here.

The reason so many people block themselves from writing, from creating, is that they are not here. They have a head full of blueprints for the goal, they have elaborate outlines of how to get there, but they have never taken a conscious walk from their bedroom to their bathroom. They want to create, but they know nothing of their own creative process. Journal writing can provide fine insights into that process.

I first began to design a journal writing course when I was a new teacher in creative writing and dissatisfied with how we taught "creative" writing. We pay so little attention to the fact that creation starts in the formless. Students come to such programs and are expected to choose a form—poetry, short story, novel. And we are so product-oriented, focusing on criticizing texts, so that they become "better poems" and "better stories." And we pay so little attention to the human beings who sit in class, their personal reasons for coming, their pain, their difficulties, what blocks them from creating, what makes them flow.

When I began to use the journal as a teaching tool in class, the writing began to flow in new ways. We were free to explore the process rather than worry about the product. Going mattered, not arriving.

SAN FRANCISCO
NOVEMBER 7
SATURDAY, 10:30 A.M.

I walked down the street last night, ding-dong, dong-ding, with my returnable bottles, to the corner store. It was late, the hour when no one walks except the dog owners. I suppose you could go for a walking meditation with your dog, as long as you are both free to stroll. But there was this man standing by the corner telephone post, and he had this huge leash and a tiny animal on it. It was one of those dogs that are no bigger than a frog, and the poor thing looked at me with its large eyes. It was shivering, trying to get its job done—its job of shitting once a day, at night, by the corner post—*and* as fast as possible, because the man was already impatient and had the leash in his hand. I wondered if that dog had ever gone down the street for a free stroll.

Writing in a journal can be like that. You can use it as a dumping place, where you dump your excrement, secretly, in the dark. And that's not good or bad, it can be helpful. For many of us, that's how we start. At least the journal is a place where we can say the unacceptable, and that helps some-times. But if we are going to keep ourselves on that big leash and be in a hurry all the time, and want to get it over with, not much will happen in that writing process.

The last few days I have been working on a thought process. It started when I read a student's text. She said when she got crayons as a child she loved it, but she always looked for the other colors. Where are the other colors?

A couple of days later I sat in the back room watching the sunset. It was an intense orange/purple, and I thought how the search for the colors is a search for certain vibrations that are familiar. We look for these vibrations not just in colors, but in words, in smells, in people.

Then I drove to class recently, and on the freeway it occurred to me that everything we experience appears in certain phenomena, and that all these phenomena are some sort of vibration pattern. (I cannot explain this in terms of science, but I can sense it.) So that anytime we make "meaning" or we are attracted, or we find one of the "other colors," we experience a familiar vibration, and we go home to something we knew, before or beyond its manifestation in this particular form.

When an artist gets excited about seeing something, feeling something, she is going home to that vibration, trying to follow it. When a mystic experiences a revelation, he is going home to a particular vibration. We are going home to the lover who embraces us, blends with us. These experiences that pull us back, or ahead, into a knowingness about something. And this knowingness we have is not tied to a form,

7

to a specific thing, but to a specific sensation. Could it be that although we recognize this sensation only when it appears in a certain form, we in fact remember it through various manifestations in and out of form? Is this how we make meaning by association, so that the "missing color" I've just found—let's say the purple of the sunset—suddenly reminds me of a polar bear in the tundra? I don't know why. Is there a homeland in the universe that constantly moves in and out of form, and are we tracking it?

I asked the students in my autobiography class how they went about selecting things to write from their life. How do they find the hot spots, the essence, the stuff that really matters? I told them that when I write I often feel like a dog, following the path, sniffing and sniffing, and when it gets exciting, intense, I start digging. When the vibration is intense, I start digging, even though I don't recognize it yet.

SAN FRANCISCO
NOVEMBER 9
MONDAY, NOON

A foggy day. Spending the day on the dark path, feeling out my own resistance. The yearning to be connected, and my unwillingness to reach out. The terrible wish to create, and my reluctance to do it. Feeling, observing, agonizing. Why am I sitting here by myself, writing, alone? The days flip-flop, from profound insight and vision, to sadness and feeling stuck. Writing is such a lonely occupation.

Dream (this morning):
I am hiking into a high mountain region. It is an area where serious climbing is being done, so all kinds of people are on their way. I arrive at a resort or chalet in the late afternoon. It is a kind of elegant base camp. There is lots of activity. Climbing teams are up in the high peak area, ready to come down. I feel an intense need to go up to the peak, the red afternoon light on the rock is pulling me. Ice in the steep crevices, but I can see a passage through.

I look at all this from the bottom, put my backpack down, then suddenly begin to climb very fast, leaving everything behind, taking only my notepad. But I stop a ways up on a natural rock ledge. I am standing in intensely red evening light, and I realize it is stupid to go up there now, and it is stupid to go with nothing but writing paper.

So I go back down and stay in the chalet. That evening at the table I say aloud, "I am going up the peak tomorrow," as if to make some solitary gesture. Then the woman to my left says, "I am coming with you." For a moment I am not sure I want that. Then the man to my right says, "I am coming also." He looks at me, a solid mountain man with light in his eyes. I realize that both of them are coming to help me, because this climb needs a team, this path needs companions, it doesn't make sense to do it alone. And I am grateful for the simple and strong way they make this clear to me.

It is always me and my solitary writing pad, reaching the high peaks alone. Perhaps some helpers came to me last night. And maybe my sense of aloneness these days has nothing to do with writing but with the many old sorrows that rise again at this dark time of the year. It is the time of year when I lost my baby. These days I am giving birth to texts rather than children. Sometimes this is very beautiful, sometimes it is very hard.

SAN FRANCISCO
NOVEMBER 10
TUESDAY, NOON

The hardest thing to do is doing what you want to do. As soon as you think of it, there are innumerable reasons why you should not do it. Writing this book, for instance. I spent a whole day on the beach arguing with myself. And all that time, the waves splashed miraculous towers onto the beach, birds ran through water tunnels and up to my feet, the white winter sun made mirrors in my face. I could have given in to this beauty and become one with my walk. But I didn't because I kept on talking in my head.

What did I talk about then? What was this voice in my head arguing, louder than the waves of the ocean? It was telling me what this journal had to be! How it had to be. What could be in it and what not. Mostly it was telling me that this project was not a good idea. The voice had very sophisticated arguments for that. It said you couldn't write a journal about journal writing because by definition a journal was . . . And I said: Whose definition? And the voice said: Yours! This hurt. I ran along the water for a while, hearing the waves splash and splash, feeling innumerable voices conspire and whisper: See, you can't do it! Stop right now. You began it the wrong way, this project. This is not the right way.

I looked at the sky through the white light and the water mist, and my chest was so constricted from all these arguments that I was amazed how birds could keep themselves in the air. Then I realized, perhaps they have no little voices in their head, telling them they can't do things. Imagine every time a bird wanted to fly, it stopped breathing long enough to think why it probably shouldn't fly. You would have a lot of lame-winged contorted creatures hopping around on the beach.

As soon as I saw that image, the air rushed into my lungs. I breathed and laughed and fell down on the wet sand and realized I had been my own torturer, built myself a little trap with my clever thoughts. A bird ran toward me, with one wing out as if lame, mocking me, and a great relief came over me at the sight of this huge ocean and all that it contained.

A journal can be anything! You hear me? A journal can be anything! This is what I told my students over and over. Listen to me: You make the rules, you make the restrictions, you give the permissions. A journal can hold just about anything. You can make it your confessional, or your g list. I suppose I could make it a textbook if I wanted. The journals I like best are treasure chests—all the things collected on the walk home, to ourselves, or on the walk out, to the other, it's all the same. You can make it your sitting practice—a daily meditation, a quiet time with yourself. I like to take mine for a walk, whether my legs move or not. My writing is a walking meditation, I find stillness in movement. My journal is a vision quest, searching for something, entry after entry, finding myself.

SAN FRANCISCO
NOVEMBER 14
SATURDAY, MORNING

A composer talked on the radio this morning, about music. He was saying that the universe communicates in sounds. The entire universe has sound to it, and that music is a representation of consciousness. He talked of the compassion of sound. As I write this down, it doesn't get across what I experienced when he talked. And the music he played didn't really express this either. But it was his words that reached me, the sound of his words.

I thought of what I wrote the other day, that everything we experience as meaning is probably a certain vibration remembered as "home," and sound would be part of that, harmonies or disharmonies.

12

When Richard first came for a visit, he asked me why didn't I play classical music. He had imagined me with classical music in the background. I explained to him that what is usually considered "good" or "elevating" music is for me just another cultural package. We experience it and immediately recognize it as important, but mostly because we have been told so. It doesn't impress me that Margaret's little girl plays Vivaldi on her violin. I would rather she tried to listen to sound that was not labeled yet—water, wind, the sound of the world.

I love sounds that come to me as sounds. I love colors that come to me as colors. They have a beingness of their own, and in the end these vibrations come to us from a place that we recognize from far beyond labeled emotions. We recognize them and turn home to them.

It is hard to use words in this way, because words, perhaps more than anything else in our culture, are prelabeled, are overused. But words, too, come as sounds, as colors, as the vibration of consciousness. It was the words of the composer that reached me and, strangely, not his music.

SAN FRANCISCO
NOVEMBER 23
MONDAY, NOON

This morning I got up at dawn, but when I was all dressed
I felt exhausted and very dreamy. So I decided to go back to
bed again and sleep. Perhaps I wasn't done dreaming. I
looked out the bedroom window, and a hawk flew by and
settled on the big pine tree, on top of it, and waited for the
sun. The light was just rising, and his head was facing east.
And I stood by the window, and then he turned his head and
looked at me. Then he turned back and waited for the sun.
So I decided to sit down and wait for the sun also.

Hawks have been everywhere where I am recently, even
here in the city. It is odd and wonderful.

I went back to bed and dreamed it was dawn, and dreamed
I was floating, weightlessly, in coral light.

Sometimes it seems as if one thing has nothing to do with
another thing, but it does. The trick is to write it down. Not
to figure it out. To write it down, one vision at a time.

I stayed home by myself today, and it felt good. Ellen called, was I coming to their house, and I said no—I was giving thanks to the great mystery that gave me this gift of writing, which I used so little, and thus I was staying home today.

We had a good talk. She said the reason she likes to have me around is that she enjoys my stories so much. She began to tell me a story I had told her about my childhood, about the house of my grandmother in the village in Austria, about the Sunday meal my grandmother cooked. And I realized I had forgotten that story. Here was a person who had never seen my childhood home or my grandmother, but the story lived in her. And I had forgotten that story and now received it back from her, my own words coming home. It was a strange feeling. I thanked her for the gift.

And later I thought: Here I am teaching all these people to write, and I don't have time to write down my own stories. Even today I am preparing to teach. Thank god for my journal. It is my daily exercise and keeps my writing voice alive.

Most people have no idea that writing takes time. I do not mean just the time that you sit at the desk, but the time it takes for dreaming the new child into manifestation. The creative process is a gestation process, and it cannot be pushed. You need time to sit around, do nothing, stare into space, dream, and play—all the while some mysterious process is going on inside you, long before you are ready to write. I call this my fiddling time. To an outsider it looks as if I am wasting the day. But to me it is the idle time I need, so I can shift realities.

Our high-paced modern life-style pushes us into an appointment book schedule that leaves little dreamtime. Even vacations and weekends are scheduled. There is no open time where life can move at its own pace. But such open space is vital for the creative process.

When I was a young girl, I could spend hours and hours in dreamtime, doing nothing in particular, just dreaming. My mother would often say to me, "Don't just sit there, do something, anything, don't just stare into space." Perhaps she didn't know about dreamtime, perhaps she was too harried with her household chores and wanted someone to help, but doing nothing was precisely what I needed to do a lot of. That's how I dreamed up many wonderful things— paintings, and poems, and life journeys.

Today I still need this idle time in order to create. Life itself is a creative process, and we need to take time for it. When we have full-time work schedules and keep busy appointment calendars, this often makes it impossible to see the slow organic process that life is, the subtle miraculous shifts that take place inside of us and around us. And without the time to observe all this, there is no writing for me. That is why I retreat on holidays and create open spaces wherever I can. And that is how the journal saves me. For a little while each day, it allows me to come home to myself, it allows me to dream, and to keep writing in small spaces of time.

Sometimes you wake up in the middle of the night and you don't know what to do with yourself. This happens often to me, and I used to agonize over it, trying every conceivable method of going back to sleep. But I don't worry about it anymore. I simply get up and begin to write in my journal, assuming that something needs to be said, or why would I wake up anxiously.

It helps if you have a fireplace with a log in it or a small heater to put next to you. If all that is not possible, putting on a warm robe might do. At any rate, journal entries at three A.M., while shivering in your nightie, don't tend to be very productive. They can of course accurately reflect the state of affairs, so if cold misery needs to be recorded, by all means do it. But I find it more helpful to be warm while writing. And I have found that these dark night hours produce some amazing journal entries that often have nothing to do with cold misery at all. One needs to be willing to write at any time, willing to try that out, without assuming to know what will happen, before one discovers what voices talk in us and at what time of day.

Last night I got up in the dark. I was already brushing my teeth before I realized that I was probably awake. But what was most amazing was not that I found myself with the toothbrush in my mouth, apparently trying to get ready for something, but that I was already halfway through writing an outline for a presentation I wanted to give sometime next spring. The sentences were rolling around in my head, precise clear statements that wanted to be put down. No wonder I couldn't sleep, the stuff was ready to come out, and so it did.

When I got to my journal, I didn't write out the presentation, because by this time that voice had stopped talking. I didn't worry about that. I made a short sketch of it and continued to write whatever came to mind. And what came to mind was a flood of ideas about next spring and summer, plans for workshops, and manuscripts to be worked on. I suddenly saw how it all could be arranged. Then I went back to bed, not sleeping but being happily slow and lazy, watching the dawn arrive. I had my work down on paper and could slide into a slow Sunday morning. By nine o'clock I was writing again, but this time in quite a different mood, watching the light of morning, making a song for myself.

By ten o'clock I began to write in this journal book, for the first time in over a month, after returning from a trip, after recovering from jet lag, after trying to reheat the icy apartment, after taking care of the mail and the bills and the urgent telephone messages, and the leaking refrigerator.

Often my writing projects have to wait until ''after'' these detours. But never my personal journal. It comes with me, and I am with it, in all those situations, on all the stations of the path, sleepy or awake, anxious or calm, on airplanes, in hotel rooms, icy or warm. It is often through the journal that I return to my other writing. It prepares me, warms up my fingers, and my words. And it is ready in the middle of the night, when the first waves of sentences suddenly surface, wanting to come out.

I don't usually keep more than one journal. Some people keep notebooks for different subjects, a separate dream journal, for instance. I advise my students to put everything in one, and I tell them: Integrate yourself! When you have everything in one journal, you can see how the fragments fit together. A dream might be a reaction to a previous event, or it might be signaling something ahead of time. Since the journal is written on a chronological time line, this becomes visible when you reread it later. If one separates things out into different notebooks, it is harder to see the larger structure of one's life process, as it slowly evolves over many entries.

SAN FRANCISCO
JANUARY 13
WEDNESDAY, EVENING

Somehow I have the feeling that I am on a strange winter journey, a long passage through darkness. That the outer dark season is only part of it. That the winter journey I took to Europe recently, and the visit to my parents' home at Christmas, were only part of it. That each of these experiences prepared me for the next turn in the long passage. One day I am very irritable, the next day strangely calm.

Before Christmas my mother called to say that my father was not well and had asked for the last sacraments. I was scheduled to be at a conference in Germany that week and had planned to be at my parents' home in Austria a few days later. My father has been ill for thirteen years, and I have flown home many times thinking that it would be the last time. All through the conference I thought: Is he really getting ready to die? Am I ready for my father's death? I don't know. Can one be ready for something like that? I have gone over all the feelings so often, over all the ways to help him or to reach out to him. In the end I can only go there and sit with him for a while, silently, because we cannot talk.

The way I talk to my father is in my journal, and in my dreams. He appears to me in dreams, and we talk about what never could be discussed in life. And I write it into my journal. Or he appears and doesn't say much in the dream, and then I write long monologues, trying to understand somehow. A few weeks ago my dreamfather appeared in a quiet sunny room. And I said to him, "Yes, I know you died, but won't you talk to me a little. Tell me how it was." He smiled a warm smile, without anger or resentment, the soft afternoon sun on his shirt and face. He said, "I hear there is talk about a journey." But he didn't tell me whose journey—his? mine? someone else's? He didn't say much, just smiled, as if it didn't matter anymore.

I think my father knows I have this connection with him in dreamtime. When I was home for Christmas, he was a little better, but still his endless suffering goes on and becomes unbearable for me. I want to reach, and there is no reaching. I need the words, and he doesn't have them. Only his agony, his anger over his pain bursts out sometimes. Then I sit there and talk to my dreamfather, or I will go to my room and write to him in my journal. Sometimes when I return he is calm, even kind. And then, a few days before Christmas, suddenly the immense gift: My father begins to tell a story about his childhood. About how he went into the mountains with his older brother. And on that day his father died. And he was a boy of only thirteen.

Sometimes this is how I feel. I feel my father died a long time ago. And so I write to him in my journal. And the words must reach him somehow. Or are they reaching me, my own words?

On the day before Christmas, my brother and I went into the mountains. We walked along icy paths, laughing and sliding, to a little chapel on a snowy hill. Then we drank coffee at a warm country inn and talked about the journey he would take soon, to Canada. He was to be the physician for the Austrian ski team at the Olympic Games. I felt at home with my brother, for the first time in years, the way we had been as children in the village, building snow tunnels in the garden. We sat at the window of the warm inn for a long time, while in the distance the avalanches were falling off the high cliffs. That evening, on Christmas Eve, my father unwrapped my present and actually smiled, before entering into darkness and pain once again.

LATER

I went for a walk to the bookstore and was drawn to the corner where the beautiful photographic books are. Opened one up, and saw a picture of a passage through ice. And knew instantly what these last few weeks have been, what this whole winter journey to Europe was—the passage through ice, at the darkest time of year.

SAN FRANCISCO
JANUARY 14
THURSDAY, EVENING

The passage through ice continues.

Today I came home with great fury, screamed at some poor telephone operator, then calmed down. The rains started. It got dark at midafternoon. I crawled into my warm nest and felt like hibernating for a long time. Tonight I read that James Cook on his voyage to Antarctica expected a lush continent but found nothing but ice.

I am making telephone calls across huge oceans and snowy continents, to a mother exhausted and desperate from years of giving nursing care to my slowly dying father. I ought to be there, but I live on the other side of the world. And inside myself, and in my journals, I travel this painful truth. Distances muffled by winter. We have the illusion in this century that we can get anyplace, reach anything, whenever we want. But I remember returning from Europe, sitting on the airplane and thinking how absurd this was, as below me passed Iceland, Greenland, Newfoundland, the North American continent, all locked in ice. I saw myself tiny, with a dogsled, trying to find my way back through continents of snow, to those I loved.

This afternoon I took a nap and woke up with a dream: *I am in an airplane with my brother, and we are landing in a desolate place of frozen dirt. No snow, just frozen earth.*

There is some passage going on inside me, at this dark time. As I write in my journal, I realize that it has never been so clear to me what winter actually is. What the cold and the dark do. How the hiding of the light affects me. How I have to face the darkness in my life, and pass through the frozen continents of my heart.

Such a passage through winter is perhaps recognized fully only in retrospect. I know I am in it, and I can only make notes in my journal. There are lapses into forgetfulness, into warmth, into anger, into delusion, into self-pity. All blur the moment, so it is often not possible to see the path step by step. But suddenly you come around the arch of an iceberg, you pass through a blue crevice into sunlight, and only then do you suddenly know you have passed through ice. And at the next step you may forget, and surface again in another month.

Sometimes one doesn't have time to write. In fact most of the time we don't have time to write. Most of the time we do not have time to be with ourselves. And when that happens, it is time for the five-minute journal entry.

First I need to notice all the reasons I do not permit myself the time: I have to go to work now, I have to take a bath first, I have to, I have to. What I really want to do is let go, let my blood flow and my breath flow, and my thoughts, and experience that calm of not being driven. The second thing I need to know is that it is possible to return to myself, to return to this flow, at any time, anywhere, even for just a short time span. A breathing meditation can teach us this, a walking meditation, but also a writing meditation.

Not having time has to do with not paying attention to the small treasures. Once you notice that five minutes here, and twenty minutes there, can be used for journal entries, your day begins to take on a different perspective. It is like walking in an open landscape, discovering the small places between the bushes where the first flowers grow after the snow, then walking on into a large meadow, then back under the trees.

This journal entry took me twenty minutes. I am so glad I wrote it before running off to work. I am so glad I reminded myself—of myself, of the day, of the spaces between the bushes. There is so much time in this daily landscape of ours.

We need to gather it like small children do, with little baskets and sticky hands.

11 A.M.

Sometimes after having found a small space to write, one finds another one that day, and another. That is because as soon as you sit down to write in the first place, something begins to flow. And it doesn't stop moving after that. It keeps on flowing through your day, forming images, forming one sentence after another. Soon you begin to listen for it, and you begin to find that many of those things you "had to do" were not that urgent after all. You become the voice that speaks inside you, and all those other things aren't half as urgent as listening to that voice and forming it on paper. You begin to sing to yourself, and soon you are walking again in that open place, which is timeless, because any time you spend in it you are at home.

The creative process is a mystical path. It is not measured in miles or minutes. It is not linear. We do not enter it after we get everything else out of the way. We must know that we can enter at any time, and anywhere. Knowing this brings an exhilarating sense of joy.

The journal is a great tool to learn about this. Take it with you, catch the scenery of the path wherever you are. Write at work, write in the streetcar, write at home. Soon you will write anywhere, whether the journal is with you or not. Soon you will walk along and realize that our daily environment is full of mysterious places. Our day, which we try so hard to separate into A.M. and P.M., into work time and sleep time, into endless have-to times, is really nothing else but an infinite number of open gates, leading to the flow of the river, leading to the path of creation. Each one of these gates is the moment you are in at present. Not in the future, not in the past, not after you wash the dishes, now! And the creative process is nothing else but the step through the open gate of now and onto the path of creation.

SAN FRANCISCO
FEBRUARY 5
FRIDAY, MORNING

What beautiful and strong powers are coming in, so often unexpected, in the middle of a passage through winter. I received a small white bear, carved of ancient walrus ivory. The Eskimo man who gave it to me said, ''Wear it on your chest.'' I feel so protected by my white bear, and I know I will surface in spring.

Then I went to a workshop where the teacher did a visualization exercise. He told us to close our eyes and to smell something that was not present. And I smelled a rose. I smelled it so strongly that I thought the room was full of roses. And the teacher explained that in our intensive smelling we were actually putting the molecules of the rose together. There was disbelief in the room, but I had to smile. I remembered the many legends of my childhood, of saints making flowers grow in winter.

Later, as I thought about this, I remembered the beautiful legend of a woman who was married to a rich and miserly man. The woman would always give things away to the poor, and her husband forbade her to do it. One day he caught her and asked her to show him what was in her apron. And as she opened her apron, it was full of roses, and he was ashamed that he suspected her and was deeply touched by her purity.

This is where the legend ends. But I thought about it a little more. Here is this woman with the gifts for the poor in her apron. Her husband catches her. He suspects an act of a lower nature, because to him her giving to the poor is a way of stealing from him. But to her the giving is an act of extreme beauty. What the woman manages to do, is focus completely on that state of beauty, and when her husband comes into that energy field, all he is able to feel is that beauty, and he sees it and smells it in the form of roses.

I was happy when I thought of this. Because I realized that this is my work. It is what I do when I write, and it is what I do when I help people understand the creative process. I am helping them to walk in beauty, and I am helping them to see—to not get stuck in the particular "meaning" of a situation, or an image, but to let the image rise, to move with it and use it in a process of transformation. Through metaphor we pass from one state of knowing into the next, ever experimenting, ever creating, ever flowing, as the universe does. It is our state of seeing that makes roses bloom—in aprons, on paper, on frozen life paths. Sometimes this state comes about through a willful creative leap, sometimes it arrives as a gift of grace.

SAN FRANCISCO
FEBRUARY 18
THURSDAY, 11 A.M.

From time to time a friend comes to my house to give me a massage. But I decided that ''massage'' is a very inappropriate word for it. I decided this should be called ''listening to the flesh.'' She touches my body, and in each place she touches, the body has stored pain and joy, memories, knowledge of many kinds. And I begin to listen—to my arm, my shoulder, my belly, the soles of my feet, my tongue, my uterus. I begin to walk in the landscape of my body, the landscape of my flesh. And I begin to write the autobiography of my flesh.

Perhaps my toe wants to tell me a story about my childhood, of the slimy places it touched, the sharp-edged stones, of the times when it still reached my mouth, toe or thumb being equally good. Perhaps my womb wants to cry the story of the child I lost, of what wanted to be formed and what slipped out into darkness before it could be held securely by the arms near the heart.

Maybe my throat wants to tell me of all the songs held

back. Held back in fear, or in doubt, or in anger, all the songs that the heart already knows but that I have not voiced. Perhaps I need to walk in that place, down my throat to the vocal cords. And maybe I need to write in my journal about the huge clump that sits there, blocking the air, blocking the sound, blocking the blood flow, causing pain. And maybe I need to discover that this big boulder sitting in my throat consists of a huge mass of words, compacted into stone— words pushed back, words too scary to face, words too tender, words too beautiful to admit. So many words wanting to be born, and all held back.

San Francisco
February 20
Saturday, 10:30 a.m.

I would say having a good place to sit is essential for writing. I have this place by the window where the sun comes in in the morning. There I sit, letting the light fall on my forehead, and from there I travel anywhere with my eyes and my ears, while my fingers walk quietly over the pages.

This is my morning ritual, my writing meditation. I return to it with pleasure. There are other places to write in, to walk in, to sit. But this place, at this particular time, for the very short span that the sun touches the table by the window, has become a gift. I delight in it. I give myself permission all the time. And it doesn't matter what I write. Returning to it, sitting here in the sun, the white pages in front of me, and the quiet scribbling. That much I know I can give myself for sure. If nothing else, that much at least.

SAN FRANCISCO
FEBRUARY 27
SATURDAY

On Thursday, February 25, my brother died in Calgary, Canada. He was run over on the ski slope by a snow-grooming machine, while on his way to a patient. It was about noon.

At that time I was walking with a friend on the beach in San Francisco. I was speaking of my brother, how proud I was of him. The wind was icy, and the beach gray. I was tired and heavy that day.

In the evening the awful phone call came. Then all drowned in a wave of terror. My breaths came as if in childbirth, like screams from way down in the womb. Not my brother? I was confused. This is the wrong death. For years I expected my father to die. But not my brother. Not my brother! This is the wrong death. They made a mistake. Not my brother.

And then the cold clarity that, yes, I had somehow known. And did not want to know. And the dreams rose in my memory from many months before. And I walked to my journal and read the dream of my brother's death.

And I froze in pain, and stared at this endless passage of ice. So much death in my life. I don't know if one can ever surface from that.

San Francisco
February 28
Sunday

The embassy in Calgary told me not to come. They said the place was a circus, everything was focused on the last days of the Olympics. There wasn't a room to be found anywhere. And nobody would have time for me. My brother's body was well taken care of.

Was taken care of? Where was he? Who was with him? I felt the agony of no one being present with his body, no one to touch him, to speak to his spirit. When I finally reached the coroner by phone, and asked should I come and identify the body, she said no, the body was so mangled one could not look at it. I asked her who was taking care of my brother's spirit, and she said, "His what?" So I only said, "Please touch him for me," and that is all I could say.

I sat in my living room and didn't know what to do. I wanted so to be close to my brother, to help him in these terrifying moments of his journey. I got out the Tibetan Book of the Dead, and began to read him the journey of the dead. It was all I knew how to do. I wanted to talk into his ear, as they had done in ancient traditions. But there was no ear, there was no body.

Then I visualized his hands being whole, his good hands that had healed so many. And so I held his hand, as I sat there, reading page after page to him, sending him on his journey.

San Francisco
March 1
Tuesday

Today my brother's body will be shipped from Canada to Austria. I have spent days making these arrangements. There were so many phone calls. I went a little crazy, as if all this pain had come in over the phone, and I never wanted to hear this machine again. I finally made reservations to fly home for the funeral, and when I was done, I felt physically ill and nauseated. I had a vision of airplanes being coffins, and me flying endlessly back and forth over a world of ice.

AUSTRIA
MARCH 8
TUESDAY

The night before my brother's funeral the sky was ivory-colored. A soft white light came from it, almost yellow, as if it held something up there in the sky that was yet of the earth. As if it were pregnant, radiating a gift of infinite calm before it gave birth.

I lay in my monk's cell, a small hotel room with white walls, overlooking an ancient courtyard. And I watched that sky all night, that cream-colored sky of my childhood. And at four o'clock in the morning it opened up and the snow came down. And the sky continued to be ivory-colored. I looked at it all night.

I had forgotten how much light is in the sky when it snows. I had forgotten about our childhood, my brother's and mine, when we knew this, and much more.

A song came to me that night. And at dawn I sang it for my brother. And I sang it at his funeral, silently inside me, sang it in the face of that frozen earth. And there was so much light around his grave that something began to soar. This song was a gift from the cream-colored sky. It is good to notice the color of things. It is good to write them down. The gifts we receive come from subtle places, when we have our eyes open, like children, open to the night sky.

ON THE AIRPLANE
MARCH 16
WEDNESDAY

Up over water again, over the Atlantic Ocean. Blue above and blue below, with icebergs dotting the below. Unreal, these travels between worlds, between different states of consciousness.

Looking into my father's face, a face that faces death, nothing but death all around—and leaving him alone, leaving, and traveling west into this dreamland of my California life. There is nothing that comforts, nothing that I can hold up for myself. I can feel a certain joy of being alive, and all the things to be seen and done in this world. I can look down from up here onto the earth, this beautiful earth. But the face of an old dying parent, left alone, stands there and asks me—about the illusions each generation has, what they will reach, what they will change and transform. Will my life's work simply be transformed again by the next generation? And will I die alone, like my father, looking back on an old world, looking on the new world of the children, finding comfort in neither? Will I find that the only thing that holds to the end is human warmth? And what if it is not there? What if your children have left, one into the grave before you, another via airplane into her brilliant illusions?

The winter journey continues, such a long, long journey. March already, and the passage continues. The white bear is sleeping in wisdom. And when the spring storms start, and when the ice breaks up, and when the bear comes out of hibernation, what will my world be like?

SAN FRANCISCO
MARCH 20
SUNDAY, MORNING

I am back in my own place, trying to stabilize. It has been a month since I last sat here quietly, at my writing table. Writing meditations are hard when life and death rip through with such force. But for me they are essential—I come home to myself and breathe.

I wrote a letter to Martin, telling him how hard it is to write a book, because everything moves so fast, it has already shifted before one gets it on paper. Death breaks in. The world races on. It is one thing to keep a private journal and to record the daily flow of life. It is another thing to write a book, to keep the focus on that essential writing process, and not drown in the flood of life events. How can I write a journal for my students and document the writing process when my daily life is being ripped open by such events?

Maybe the truth is that the creative process works in all these places, and everything that breaks into one's life is part of it. Perhaps only in a journal can one see how life and art intertwine and are really only one great journey.

Yesterday, after I returned from Europe, I drove out to the coastal hills, through oak and bay trees that I so love, and the green California winter. But I got terribly confused and exhausted—is it winter, is it spring? Who is in the grave, who is alive?

My friends were building a sweat lodge. I touched the earth, but nothing seemed real. The Eskimo man came and talked to me. He told me the story of how his two boys went fishing in Alaska, and how the ocean took them, his only two sons. He said when we lose someone we love, there is a terrible vacuum that forms, but because of it we recognize all other things coming toward us.

The sweating was difficult for me that day. I wanted so much to release all that pain from my body, but I had a hard time letting anything flow. Finally I put my chest and my belly on the earth, and I had a vision of my brother's grave. I kept saying, "Rise up, come out," and then I realized what a spiritual being the earth is, full of spirit. We always visualize the spirit in the air, and so we try to raise the dead out of their graves. But suddenly I saw how spirit is through all of the earth. How light the earth forms are when you realize this. And the image of his grave became filtered with lightness, and I understood that we can filter into life when we are in the womb of the earth.

SAN FRANCISCO
MARCH 22
TUESDAY, MORNING

Dream:

I am standing on a mountain slope facing south and looking downward. Behind me is some sort of building. I have just walked out of there and am exhausted by something, unable to do much. And suddenly there is a wild rush from behind me. Coming by on my right side is a group of black bears, running by me, and breaking through the brush, and down the hill in a wild spring rush.

I guess this is the end of hibernation, of the winter journey, and I am in for a turbulent awakening. The truth is, I am exhausted every day and can barely teach my classes. But I do have strength for writing. Perhaps it gives me life energy. The daffodils are blooming in the park. It is almost Easter.

SAN FRANCISCO
MARCH 26
SATURDAY, EVENING

I want to talk about judgment, the judgment that looks over our shoulder when we write. Or the judgment that smirks in our face when we feel something so deeply, but the moment we consider writing it down, it seems bizarre and embarrassing. Or the judgment that we imagine will be delivered to us once we submit our writing to the proper authority (whoever that may be—our parents, teachers, an editor, or society in general). And I want to say: Throw out any judge that appears, imaginary or physical, in the same room where you write. But I know how hard that is.

One reason journals are such fine tools to learn about the creative process is that a journal is rarely considered a final literary form while one writes it (although it certainly can be). A journal is a private fragmentary scribble book. It doesn't have to "be" anything specific, and so it is easier to give yourself permission to "fail." And "failing"—that is, writing without wanting to produce a certain form and without wanting to achieve a certain result, seemingly giving up intention and seeing what comes of it, learning from the process as it unfolds—is a great way to learn about the creative process. This is a mystical path. You walk on it daily without knowing what will come tomorrow. But you trust, by writing down the daily fragments of awareness, that a larger network will gradually emerge, that images will come forth, a theme or direction may appear, all of which you could never have outlined, but which emerge out of deep necessities within us. Trusting that inner necessity—not defining it prematurely, not curbing it, but looking at the odd child that is born out of us, without fear, learning from it—is to stay in the flow of creation.

Judgment has to do with imposing form on something that may still be in motion, labeling it, fixing it in some aspect, and thus controlling it before it has a chance to grow into its own wholeness.

Students often come to me and say they are afraid that their writing is "self-indulgent," a label that will surely stop dead any attempt of trusting their inner necessity. I tell them perhaps it is quite necessary to "indulge" in the "self" in order to learn what emerges from the self and how it forms and creates. In writing classes, students are often encouraged to practice "criticizing" each other's texts from the first day on, trying to make "better" poems and stories, pushing them into shape, imposing some sort of standard, pronouncing judgment on what the text "is," and often also on the person who wrote it. All the while we don't see that many of these texts are fragments in motion, and that they and their creators are on the way somewhere. And all that our judgment often does is stop that motion in midflight and fix that text into a distorted final form. I sometimes think that we would do better not to practice so much criticism but rather learn through years of patient observation.

This is also true of our own writing process. I always tell myself: Observe and observe what comes out of you, but don't let anything stop you from writing it, and don't destroy it until you have let it sit for good long time and until you have gotten used to its strangeness or its embarrassment. Don't stop the words coming out of you. Rather, curb the need for constant approval, for being instantly famous, for producing the perfect text tomorrow. Enjoy the walk on the path! Sometimes, and for some writers, there will indeed be some great reception on the way. And it is nice to be honored for something one did well. But it's the process and discovery on the way that is the true excitement. The journal writer can hardly ever count on great receptions along his or her path of writing. And so it becomes a lovely process by itself. No approval, no judgment, only an ever-growing awareness of the self in motion.

A few weeks ago I was talking to the priest who buried my brother. This was a very unusual man, and I had come to thank him for taking so much care preparing this last ritual for my brother. We were talking about death, and he said, "The Final Judgment is not at all what most people think it is. It doesn't mean to judge someone, but rather it means to see things, to set them right, within a different perspective, as they truly are, in the immense light of the divine. To die is to come home to that, and the Final Judgment is that Seeing."

If we could practice that "Seeing" a little, while we are still alive, our art and our teaching of it would be profoundly different.

KLAMATH FALLS
MARCH 30
MONDAY, EVENING
AT SUNSET

Sometimes there is a day so beautiful that one cannot write more than a few lines. I saw eagles today, so many eagles flying in and out of and above the marshes of the wildlife refuge.

I have come here before, to this place of the birds. This year I came to find refuge myself, from heaviness and grief. I came tired and undecided but with something driving me on. This year I kept saying, "I want to see one eagle."

The first eagle I didn't see, it saw me. It flew straight at me. A bald eagle, it flew straight at me with its white head and its black wings spread out. I said, "My god, that's an eagle," and it kept flying toward my eyes as if to say, "Now do you finally see me?" After that they kept coming, all day long, until I stopped counting—golden eagles, bald eagles, soaring. So many birds. Hawks, so many. At one time I looked through the binoculars and had an eagle, a hawk, and a great blue heron all in my picture at the same time, coming toward me.

Snow geese in long strings of pearl against the mountains in the background. Snow geese, thousands upon thousands, a white blanket settling on Thule Lake. Mount Shasta in snow, in full volcanic majesty, shimmering in the background. I love this earth.

Now, in the evening, I sit by the window, look out at the

mountain, close my eyes, and hundreds of wings come toward me. So many wings inside me, a heart full of wings, arms, toes, brain, tongue, all wings. And a huge motion goes through me, and we travel together.

SAN FRANCISCO
APRIL 10
SUNDAY, MORNING

Sometimes there is a great impatience in us. I wake up in the morning, and it feels as if I am already too late for everything, no matter how early I got up. It feels as if I need to run somewhere, my body already racing there. I don't really know where "there" is, but at any rate I can feel that "here" is not here and I run "there" to find it.

This week I walked into my journal writing class, and the whole class was in that state. It felt like walking into a practice room for race drivers, or something like that. This is usually when I announce a present moment exercise. And so I did, and things calmed down a bit, and I was "here," and most of the people in the classroom were then "here," and we could proceed with writing.

A present moment exercise is often done in meditation. You simply sit quietly somewhere and become aware of the present moment—the place you sit in, your breathing, your body and all its muscles and organs. And you try to be simply "here," aware of the "now," and you feel it, this "now," rather than racing off into thoughts about tomorrow or what happened yesterday, or what else you have to do.

I begin many of my writing classes and many of my own journal entries with this exercise. In class I often tell my students to get up, perhaps go outside, find a place to sit that feels just right for now, and feel the present moment in that place for a few minutes. Then to come back to class and write from that experience, or stay at that place and write there. It is usually a short exercise, but it often changes the tone to a calmer and yet very alert state of being. And it makes us ready for creating from this moment—I am here, I am writing.

Several years ago I devised a daily exercise for myself, and I often tell this to my students to show them that the present moment is never the same. Each moment is a new one, a new revelation, no matter how often you sit down in the very same place. And when you become aware of that, you realize the wealth of daily experience, the wealth you have for writing, for creating, at any moment.

The exercise I devised for myself was to get up every day at the same time and sit in the same chair in front of the same window and write there. I did this for about six months— precisely the same place in front of the same window. It looked out on a beautiful hill with horses grazing on it. I wanted to know if one would run out of things to say, always writing in the same place at the same time.

And I discovered that the present moment comes in infinite variations and that a lifetime would not be enough to record the endless interplay of hill and horses and sky and light and window and myself. Most of all I became aware of myself in that exercise, and my journal of those six months became a discovery of the strange being I was—ever shifting from moment to moment, fluctuating with emotions and memories. And I noticed the hill was different when I was dark, and it was different when I was light. And on the other hand, when I was dark, sometimes the hill would present me with this lovely gift of light I had not expected. And this interchange gradually began to grow into a sense of trust, a complete trust in whatever came toward me in the present moment, and I began to use it as a gift for writing. Not to get up in the morning and already have something in mind, not to sit down and expect something to happen, but to sit down and see what there is today, in this moment, inside myself and outside myself. And always to be ready for the gifts that come, but not to plan them.

Sometimes the horses would stand there and laugh at me, at my earnestness with this task. Then I would put my pen down and go for a long walk on the hill.

There are days when I feel very gray. The fog comes in from the ocean and seems to melt into my bones. And my journal becomes a cold and desolate landscape. I ride in it and notice my aches and pains. I ride through my sorrow, my disappointment. I am a dark knight on a dark horse. This, too, is part of the path. Let no one tell me that it isn't, or that it shouldn't be.

On some days the fog builds into a raging storm. The knight goes into full battle armor, rides into a dark forest, struggling wildly with dense growth, with dragons and beasts. My own mother may be under attack, or a friend. Pain carries the blazing banners of righteousness, and sometimes I ride with it on my steaming horse: "Why doesn't she ever understand me?"

Not even the dead are safe from these battles, "Brother, why didn't you call when you said you would? We could have talked one more time, and . . ."

The journal listens and listens. The fog rises from the swamps. The knight rides through a dark place, and that, too, must be written. We carry a wilderness inside us, and we know so little about it.

My first journals were timid attempts to chart some pathways into that wilderness. And that task is perhaps never completed in one's lifetime. It takes a lot of courage to look at one's inner swamps, to battle it out with the monsters that have lived there for a long time, since childhood perhaps. When we go on a quest, we usually set out imagining that we will find beautiful things—treasures, and power, and magic visions. The truth is that when you enter unknown territory, and you carry with you a map that has only the beautiful places on it, you are bound to face some ugly mudholes somewhere. And so it is with journal writing. One day we have large revelations, the next day we are stuck in old pain. But if we keep writing, eventually some sort of map does emerge, a map of our own wilderness.

This map, however, is not fixed but fluid. In my own journals I saw that, after years of writing, things began to change. Perhaps the knight changed, perhaps the landscape did, or the language I used. Who knows? At any rate I noticed that the charts and maps I now make of my inner wilderness are different. Some benevolence has entered, a deep affection for those unknown territories, some strange conversion of danger into beauty. I may still be the knight riding through a dark place, but I am also the journal writer observing the scene with compassion. And more often than not I end up making love to the wild beasts, to the strange light that is suddenly shed onto unknown things.

5 P.M.

What I noticed in my early journals, and what I see often with my students, is how much we use the language, the charts and maps of psychology, when we want to explain our lives. In this century we have gotten so used to the language and explanations of psychology that we don't even notice it. Many people's journals are nothing but endless attempts at finding psychological explanations for their life and for the people around them. And yet the maps and images of the self that psychology has so far presented to us are often severely limiting, in that they fail to represent large areas of human experience and the infinite variations of cause and effect within our lives.

There are other languages, other maps, that can be used in the writing process, and they have been used for centuries. In recent years a flood of spiritual publications—and thus other maps of consciousness and with it another language— has become available to us. And now one can observe writers making very sudden conversions in terms of the language they use, and one can even identify the new spiritual path they are walking by the new language they have chosen. Sometimes I come across journals where this conversion from standard Western psychology into some new spiritual map took place with such speed that one wonders about the depth of such transformations, and one sees it reflected in a language of platitudes. This can also be true of people who go through recovery programs or any of the many self-improvement trainings offered today. Their language can become the language of converts, their journals affirmations of the training, and the map of their inner wilderness is often not their own but charted by the program. This does not mean that people who go through such transformations shouldn't keep journals. On the contrary, these can be the most fertile times for writing. But the language we use must become our own and not the ready-made phrases of a pre-scribed path.

Developing a language of one's own, with distinct colors and nuances, with maps and charts and images that voice the self, takes a long time. It is a writer's lifelong work. And the journal is a patient tool in that process.

The language I used at the beginning of today's entry—the knight that battles dragons and beasts—is a language borrowed from mythology. In some ways a writer's struggle to develop his or her own language is also a struggle to develop a mythology of one's own. And this mythology, its images and its language, may, in the time we live in today, be borrowed from many parts of the world, but it must become deeply grounded in one's own life. Then the journal becomes not just a record of the path walked but the creation of a new mythological landscape.

The mythologist Joseph Campbell once said, "No one can give you a mythology. You don't have one, you are in the process of making one, and your life will be your mythology. The images that mean something to you, you find in your dreams, your visions, in your creative work, you find them in your actions, and you find out what they are after you passed them."

11:00 P.M.

Tonight we had an extra meeting for my autobiography class, to make up for the time I missed when I left for my brother's funeral. The two older black women were there, and I was glad to see them, such fine women.

Everyone read stories of death. It must be some strange way of giving me a gift in my sorrow. Showing understanding. And I took it as such. Some of these stories took much courage to write, and they had never been told.

One of the women brought me a small red rose "from Carl's rosebush." She read the story of her son Carl who got into drugs and committed suicide by jumping from a tower. I held the coral-red rosebud in my hands and loved her for this gift.

SAN FRANCISCO
APRIL 18
MONDAY, 4:30 P.M.

Today it is raining. It is raining in a drought year. Usually when it rains in California, most people are slightly annoyed, as if they were entitled to an endless series of blue-skied days and as if the rain had messed it all up. Those of us who live here but grew up in wetter climates find this attitude a little amusing, perhaps even disturbing. Maybe some of us also moved here for the blue and sunny days, but then we realized how much we missed the rain, how we missed its smell, and its sound, and its everything. We become rain worshippers, and in a year of severe drought even the regular Californian may join us and say thanks when it is wet.

For me such days have become celebrations, even when there is a whole series of them. When I wake up in the morning and hear the sound on the roof, when I look out the window and know by the color of the sky and the clouds coming in from the ocean, that it will be a rainy day, I am happy, and begin my celebration. I may cancel an appointment, I may change the whole day around, or I may go about my day with its scheduled routine but with a secret sense of joy inside me. The celebration of a rainy day may include walking outside. It usually includes long sessions of journal writing in a cozy, warm place looking out into the wet, but most of all it includes many small moments during the day, becoming aware of my joy, of the pleasure of water, of the beauty of our environment when it is altered slightly and we notice it. And these many small moments can become a continued writing meditation, without pen, without paper, just noticing.

6 P.M.

Today I opened a book on walking meditation. It talked about the miracle of walking on earth, how we manifest this in each of our steps. It said to think of your foot as an emperor's seal.

I saw myself walking, on the wet ground, putting my seal down, step by step, imprinting the earth with my celebration. And all the small moments of awareness during the day became invisible seals in my mind. I saw myself walking across the white pages of my journal, imprinting it with my small moments of revelation.

I have a confession to make. A writing celebration can be done on any day. In fact, I do it quite often on brilliantly sunny days, journal in hand.

Sometimes the foggy days give me difficulty. Perhaps in time I'll be able to appreciate them also. Perhaps those difficult entries in our journals, when we seem to walk through a desolate land, imprinting page after page of pain in the book of our life—perhaps those, too, carry the royal seal. Sometimes we recognize this years later. We find a page in a journal from many years before, and suddenly we recognize the terrible beauty of a difficult passage through ice.

San Francisco
April 22
Friday, morning

Dream (yesterday):
I am with my mother, going shopping in some of the small stores down the street. We enter a store and something is shown to us, something very white. First there is no image, just a glittering whiteness. Then it forms into the image of white fur, and then it seems there is a rabbit, no, a large white hare on the table. The shopwoman takes the hare, and suddenly I realize she is going to

slaughter it. I leave the place immediately. I am terribly upset
because this beautiful animal is so alive with its sparkling white fur.
Then the rabbit is dead, and the bloody carcass is presented to me.
I keep saying, "You can't do this, you can't do it this way." And
I begin to make a prayer over the animal, blessing the four directions.
I am aware in the dream that I am using an ancient ceremony in
an environment where that is not normally done. But I feel deeply
the need for a prayer, as if the animal had been killed in a way that
was wrong. And I bless the animal and pray in all four directions
around the body.

I was very startled by this dream yesterday, so much that
I had trouble writing it down. I was terrified by the slaughter.
But there was something about that white fur that was myste-
rious, as if it kept on talking to me.

In the afternoon I went for a walk in the park and for some
reason was very drawn to the Asian Art Museum. They had
an exhibition of Asian embroidery which I wasn't really that
interested in, but then I went in anyway. And as I walked in,
there was the robe of a Taoist priest. It had golden medallions
embroidered on the back, and as I looked closer, on the right
shoulder a medallion with a white hare in it. There was a
note below explaining that this was "the white hare pounding the elixir of immortality." I went home and wrote that
into my journal. And I thought of that radiant white fur of
my dream, and I grew calmer.

SAN FRANCISCO
APRIL 24
SUNDAY, AFTERNOON

I keep dreaming and dreaming. So many dreams, I can't write them all down, so many each night.

I am dreaming of babies: *Babies are coming to me. Animal babies, human babies. I find them, I carry them, they are magic. Today I dreamed I found two cougar babies, twins, in my garden.* I woke up and cried as I remembered the dream I had had the night before my brother's death: *I was a panther, running in the woods with my twin, and there was danger, a terrible danger coming toward us.*

In my dream today the little cougar twins were so beautiful. They came out of the earth, then disappeared into a tree. I feel that I saw something very sacred. Perhaps life is reborn.

SAN FRANCISCO
APRIL 29
FRIDAY, 3 P.M.

When I was a small child I thought with the language of colors. As soon as I went to school and learned about letters and numbers, I perceived them as colors too. Soon I was doing my arithmetic by color combination, and this worked very well for a while. I could also remember the spelling of simple words by remembering the color combination of the letters. One would think that such abilities would help a child tremendously. In fact, the opposite happened. The first year of school was a great success, perhaps due to these abilities, or perhaps due to other circumstances, I don't know. But after that each year became more difficult. For one, I didn't recognize what secret code I was using, and neither did anyone else.

It was many years later that a poem flooded out of me one day, in the middle of a journal entry that was seemingly on something else, and there on the page was a strange color code, as if someone had dictated it and I had nothing to do with it. After that, memory after memory came back to me, from that small child I had been, a child that had listened to the universe and understood much—the code of colors, the vibration of light and sound, the grammar of taste and smell—understood much, but when she began to translate this into the code of school, something didn't work. Numbers were patient for a while, but teachers were not. Over and over they tried to impress on her mind the correct spelling of words, the correct grammatical use. But she did not listen to them. She didn't like their color combinations, and she didn't like their sound combinations, and they knew nothing of the grammar of the universe. She could make beautiful words, she could make beautiful pictures, horses talked to her, and the snow, and the gray mud by the river.

One day when the child was eleven years old, a woman appeared in class, an old woman. She read stories to the class, strange stories with a beautiful rhythm, about Baldur's horse hurting its foot. And then this teacher said, "Now you write." And when the young girl read her story about the horse, the old woman looked at her and smiled, and the young girl knew this was the first time someone understood the same language. The old woman didn't come back, and after that it was many years before the girl saw that smile of recognition again. But by then she was a woman and had been talking to paper for a long time.

4:30 P.M.

Talking to paper is talking to the divine. It is talking to an ear that will understand even the most difficult things. Paper is infinitely patient. It will receive small fragment after fragment of a large network you are working on, without you yourself knowing it. It will wait out decades for you to put together the first faint traces of your own code, a code you might have understood as a small child but which you are now gathering on a new level of understanding. The white paper is waiting. Each time you scratch on it, you trace part of yourself, and thus part of the world, and thus part of the grammar of the universe. It is a huge language, but each of us tracks his or her particular understanding of it.

SAN FRANCISCO
MAY 1
SATURDAY, NOON

This morning I walked into the kitchen and a shaft of light hit
the table, it filled the large clay bowl with the four lemons
in it. The light from above, the glaze of the earthen bowl
reflecting it, and the intense yellow of the lemons radiating
it back out. It was like an exquisite prayer. I stood there for
a while, folding my own hands into quiet attention. There is
nothing to be said about this except to notice the incredible
beauty with which objects reveal themselves to us.

When I begin a new journal writing class, I often shock my
students with my first exercise. It is a very simple exercise,
and yet many people have never done it. They have never
really looked at an object. They may have kept journals for
years, thinking that they kept records of their daily lives, but
they never included in those records the objects that touch
their lives at every moment of the day.

I simply take a chair, an ordinary classroom chair, put it
in the middle of the room, and say, "Look at it for a few
minutes, then write from that experience." Some want to
write immediately. But I tell them, "No, look for a while,
then write." Some find this very uncomfortable. Some find
it silly. Some complain that the chair is ugly. Occasionally
someone walks out, saying that this isn't a journal writing
class. And then there are students who are thoroughly delighted because they realize instantly that they had never
thought about including this sort of material in their journals,

and that they were just given permission to do so. Journal writers tend to focus on their inner world and they tend to think that the outer, physical world has little to do with that.

How much the outer has to do with the inner, and the inner with the outer, how much the inner forming of concepts and understandings has to do with the outer images we see, how much a writer's training has to do with recognizing this—all this is a long process of learning. I simply begin by saying, "Observe the chair." Some people will write an exact physical description of the chair, others will immediately identify with the chair and make it human, writing about the feelings of the chair, and others will use the chair as a metaphor, a symbolic image that can be used to express some other insight. When these texts are read aloud, none of them is right or wrong or good or bad. The writers all learn from one another in that they recognize that each writer made a choice how to relate to, and write about, the outer object, and that this choice was directly related to his or her inner self.

For each one of these choices there is a number of published texts one can read as examples. Scientists, naturalists, and travelers often focus their journals on the outer world. Yet in a strange way they often come to some profound inner understanding through the process of these outer journeys. The exploration of a strange animal, or continent, or phenomenon in the universe, can also become an exploration of the self in its relationship to these things. A journey that seemingly goes away from the self—out to the objects, the plants, the animals, the many silent things in the world—

becomes in the end the discovery of a new continent, a new language on this globe called the Conscious Self.

I usually send my students home on that first day of class with instructions to go out into the world of things, to see them everywhere: to look, to listen, to write. And they usually come back with treasure boxes, with a new awareness of what a journal can be, but most of all with a delight in the fullness of the world around them, in the mystery of the daily things that touch us. They come back with an astonishment over how much material for writing they had left out. "Chairs will never be the same again," a woman once wrote to me. And neither will her writing.

But the lesson with the chair has only just begun. The next time I put a chair in the middle of the classroom, I say, "Now let the chair look at you." At this point some people may seriously object, mumbling that this has definitely nothing to do with writing, that some strange occult things are being practiced in this class and that they are going to complain to the administration. This happens rarely. But many people are very uncomfortable with this exercise. They simply do not know how to handle it, and often the only way they can deal with it is through humor, inventing sarcastic little statements which the chair might utter about humans.

There are mystical traditions where this reversal of seeing is practiced as a meditation exercise. But for many people in our modern world it is almost inconceivable to think that they might be looked at by anything else around them except humans and perhaps some animals. Modern human beings have developed a terrible arrogance by assuming that they are the only ones who can see, perceive, observe, and understand anything in the world around them. Perhaps we make some exceptions for animals, but when it comes to trees, rocks, clouds, mountains, and especially the so-called dead and man-made objects, we draw the line. How could the chair possibly look at us? We are the conscious beings! It is not! And yet it is precisely this attitude which points to the limitation of our consciousness.

Every poet has practiced this reversal of seeing to some extent without necessarily being trained in a mystical tradition, and often without being aware of it. Children do it all the time. Painters do it, and musicians. A good scientist will practice it. It is sometimes labeled intuition. It has to do with listening, letting the thing tell you about itself, through its color, its sound, its movement, its way of being. It has to do with not imposing yourself on the thing. Letting it look at you, letting it reveal itself in its otherness, different from your assumptions. It has to do with being receptive to the unknown language of things, learning little by little from the way they show themselves to us.

This is when the journal becomes more than a friend or a confessional, more than a record of our daily events and feelings. This is when the journal becomes a network of revelations, both the revelations received from listening and observing, and the insights that come from writing this down. And sometimes upon rereading such a journal the greatest of all revelations happens, the realization that these snatches one has recorded, seemingly at random, add up to a new understanding, a new something one begins to grasp.

Once, when I walked on a mountain, a dream came back to me that I had dreamed a long time ago. I sat down under an oak tree, and a breeze came up and it was as if it carried me back to myself. The breeze came up the slope of the mountain, and the images came back to me one by one. It occurred to me then that my life was stored in some strange journal somewhere, in fact that I was the journal. That I was the journal, and that which was stored in it, and the person who kept it, all at once. Except that I knew so little about it. I was the mountain and I was the wind, carrying my own scent back to me. I was the oak tree who dreamed the mountain and the wind and all the other images that came in on the breeze, but I knew so little about myself. I didn't know where I was rooted, or where my lungs lived that breathed out these images and then breathed them in again. I wanted to retrace my steps, see if I could find back to myself. And so I began to write down my dreams.

The first journal I ever kept was a medical journal, many years ago. It was actually not a journal but some notes I jotted down on a calendar about my physical condition. I was always sick, constantly in pain, but when I got to a doctor's office, nobody could ever tell what was the matter with me. I didn't trust doctors: Who were these strange creatures who couldn't feel what I felt? I decided that I would make my own exact observations about my body and would keep daily notes on how I felt, what I ate, what I did.

The calendars had very little space to write in each day, and soon I had to buy little notebooks to be able to write it all down. Especially the "how I felt" took a great deal of time to write down, and my notebooks got larger and larger. Then one day I was faced with a difficult decision. I realized how much pleasure this daily rhythm of writing myself down gave me. The notebook was really the only "person" to whom I could freely say all these things, the notebook knew my body better than any doctor had ever known it, or any lover. And the notebook began to know a lot of my feelings. I realized that I was actually beginning to keep a diary, but I didn't like diaries. They were for young girls, I was over thirty by then. And they were for sentimental people who write all that embarrassing stuff down, and then one day someone finds it and reads it, and then all posterity knows. A horrible thought. But the arguments didn't last very long. The pleasure of writing was too great, and by then I had also reached a point where I knew that the pain was not just in my body. And I knew that it wasn't a matter of looking for the pain, or for the cause of it, but that I had discovered what an amazing creature I was, and I couldn't stop myself from discovering her.

By the time I began to write down my dreams consistently, I was using beautiful large blank books, the ones artists use for sketching. And that's what I did. I thought of myself as someone who sketched everything. I still did my daily medical sketch on myself. I sketched my dreams. I sketched my feelings. And I began to sketch the outdoors.

I lived in the backcountry by myself then. The journal was my only companion. I took it everywhere on my long walks into the open land, and we saw the mysteries of the earth together. It began to be a notebook with field notes, but strange field notes—about the hawk I saw in the meadow, and the hawk I saw in my dream. Something began to come together. Something about inner and outer. One image with another image. Little by little my pain became less. The dreams kept coming, even by day, even out on my walks. First I didn't know what to call these dreams that came in the middle of the day. First I called them poems, but later I simply called them visions, and by then I knew it didn't matter whether they came at night or by day. They were part of the same map. I walked in my own wilderness, and I walked in the wilderness of the mountain, and I knew that the journal had taken me to a place of health where no doctor could have.

SAN FRANCISCO
MAY 7
SATURDAY, 10:30 A.M.

Sometimes in journal classes the strangest things happen. A young woman came to class in the spring of last year. She was always a little angry, and I encouraged her to write about this. Angry about her mother, angry about her father, a little angry about her husband, angry about herself. A little angry about the class, a little angry about me, the teacher. I remembered that anger well from my own life. It's a feeling like waking up in the morning and finding that nothing ever quite fits in this world. Most of all finding that oneself doesn't fit. Fit what? One really isn't sure, but one has that constant feeling of never being right somehow.

As the weeks went by, the young woman, along with the rest of the class, became a little calmer. I gave weekly writing assignments in the form of themes, and the students were to focus their journal entries during the week on those themes, using them as guidelines. One week they were encouraged to discover the objects around them, another week they were to pay attention to their dreams. One week I asked them to look at the outer landscape, another week at their inner landscape. The students were never forced to write about anything, their journals were theirs. The themes were merely there as a focus.

After a few weeks such a class usually settles into a rhythm of writing, a rhythm of experiencing and writing around those themes. And when they come to their weekly class meetings, there is great excitement—reading some of their entries aloud and comparing what someone else has experienced and written about during the week. And this rhythm of living, writing, and sharing with others, usually becomes a deeply comforting feeling, something many people never had in their lives before. Going out for weekly explorations, into the outer world, and into the sphere of one's own consciousness, and then coming back to the consciousness of the group, having a circle of people and being able to compare what they experienced, and how they perceived it, and how they wrote it down. All this creates a sense of trust and companionship. It also creates an expanding awareness of the reality in all these different lives, of each person's perception—how it is different, how it is similar to one's own. And needless to say it is invaluable learning for a writer, to see and compare how each one of these conscious human beings puts a similar experience into a totally different form of language.

What tends to happen after a while in such a class atmosphere, in such a rhythm of living, and writing, and exchanging, is that people lose their fear—their fear of not being right somehow. They begin to delight in the great variety of phenomena in this world, inner and outer, the beauty of the difference in human beings, and the beauty of the many ways they express their consciousness in language. And from then on the rhythm of exploring and writing becomes a path of mysteries unfolding to be seen. And the initial anger and fear of not being right somehow, turns into a sense of wonder and amazement about all that one is just beginning to discover.

At about the time when the class had just reached that stage, when the angry young woman had become calmer, and when it was just beginning to be a beautiful spring outside, I gave an assignment to the class: ''This week pay attention to the strangers that come into your life. Pay attention to the unknown, the new and the strange, and write about it in your journals.'' The class went home and came back the next week. The young woman didn't come to class for a while but came back several weeks later. She walked in and looked at me, saying, "You and your assignments about strangers coming into our lives. You know what? I am pregnant! What are you, a witch?"

There was great excitement in the class over this news. There was laughing and joking, and there were questions. Finally everyone settled down enough for the young woman to read her journal entries to us. And others read their entries from the week when they observed the new and unknown coming into their lives. We heard some wondrous observations, but the news about the baby that had been conceived—that something "real" and physical had seemingly come out of a writing assignment—this news stayed on top of the list of excitements. But a lingering suspicion remained for a while, and a question directed at me, the teacher: How could that be?

What did I say? I don't remember exactly. What could I say except to talk a little bit about receptivity? That the mental and the physical are not separate. That when you are open to the miracles of the world, you are open on all levels. I remember making a little joke which broke the suspicion that I could cause such things to happen. I said, "Look, I asked you to pay attention to the stranger—I didn't ask you to invite him in. That was your decision." There was much laughing about that, and the class settled down. But that little stranger, that growing baby, stayed with us in class. As the weeks went by, the young woman read many journal entries to us—about her doubts of having a child when she herself had barely begun to discover herself, and about the amazing new growth that was taking place inside her. Her awareness changed and her journal changed, became ever more conscious of the subtle shifts in her and around her. And slowly her language changed and became simple, condensed—small entries, clear images, poems, meditations. And we grew with her. We all changed in our awareness of the writing process, of the strange and mysterious things that grew out of us.

Recently that class had a reunion. The young woman came with her baby and put it into my arms. We all held that child, every one of us. Then the young woman read from her journal one more time. She was moving to a different part of the country and would not see us again. And she said, "What I learned in that year with my journal was how magical everything is and that I can take this sense of the miraculous with me wherever I go." She didn't want to leave, but she had learned to use her journal as a chart for new territory and she would be all right. We talked to the beautiful little stranger she had invited into her life, and the little one looked at us and smiled. And no one asked anymore how that could happen. We all had learned that when you become conscious of something, your world changes. The journal was merely a tool in that process. But for many in that circle the writing had also become a birthing process, bringing forth not only a new concept of self but also many new and beautiful creations in language.

Yesterday I went to a sweat lodge ceremony. It happened to be Mother's Day, and as I sat in the dark lodge I realized that I was sitting in a womb. I was sitting in a womb with all my thoughts and feelings, with my head and my belly and my limbs, but no one would recognize me until I emerged. Then suddenly someone asked me to sing a song. There, in the dark lodge, I sat and sang my song. Sang my song, and I wasn't even out of the womb yet. And all could hear it and began to sing with me. And I realized that all our creations come out of us before we recognize our full birth. We are wombs within wombs and bring forth in the dark. And all that we create is our child.

And my journal is such a womb. I sit in it with my limbs and my belly and my thoughts and my dreams. But I sit in the dark for a long time and don't recognize that I have already given birth to myself—until a song comes out of me, a dream, a vision, a sudden flash of recognition of my own wholeness. And I realize that all along I have been giving birth to my creations, my text children, even while I did not recognize my own shape yet. And I continue to collect myself, my skin, my color, my voice, my shape. And each time I gather something, it is also my creation, is also my child.

SAN FRANCISCO
MAY 10
TUESDAY, 11 A.M.

I want to talk about images. The images that come to us and tell us things. Sometimes they come from inside, and sometimes they come from outside. One needs to pay attention when they come. And one needs to receive them without too much questioning at the time. Listening to them, so to say, as one can listen to an object, or to the wind, or to the sun as it enters a room.

Before I write down my dreams, I first listen to them. I treat myself gently as I wake up, not jumping out of bed, just keeping my eyes half-closed and listening to the images of the dream as best as I remember them. Not pushing the dream into a story that has to make sense, just gently looking at the images that surfaced. And then with my eyes still closed, I begin to sketch them, as a painter would. Not questioning, not interpreting, just making a sketch inside myself, so that I remember the dream like a photograph. And when I get up, I put the sketch into my journal, in writing. Sometimes I also draw or paint the picture into my journal. But when I write it down, I write as fast as I can, not questioning, because in the transfer from image to language, much can be lost if one thinks about it too much. I write as fast as I can, not thinking, not interpreting, just recording what I saw, so that I can listen to it later, as close to the raw form in which it came. So that I can listen to the images without having smothered them in my quick opinions.

Dreams are not necessarily stories, and they are rarely predictions, although they certainly can be. Dreams sensitize us to what we are then able to perceive in the waking state. It is almost always the image, rather than the story line, which carries the "message," although it can also be a sensation, a sound, even a smell. So any fraction of a dream one can catch is good. That is the message that has managed to reach me that day, and that is what I will listen to. Sometimes, if one keeps holding such a dream image during the day, or even for a longer time, other information will come from the outside world and add on to the "meaning." The point is not to go around and look for meaning, or to consult some dream interpretation book, or to immediately ask for someone else's opinion. The dream came to you, and it is your task to listen, and your privilege to be enlightened by it. Sometimes I carry my dream images in gestation for a long time, and as I walk through my days with them, the world around me behaves like a godmother, adding this and that little gift to the crib, and the image grows in me, until one day perhaps I recognize its origin.

A few weeks ago when I dreamed of a white hare, I didn't want to write down the dream. There were only a few images that I remembered clearly, and one of them was terrifying—of slaughter. I had trouble writing it down, because I kept thinking of my brother's fatal accident, and the image was unbearable. But what remained with me most insistently, after I did write it down, was the vibration of the white hare's fur. It was shining and radiant. I had never seen fur like this and later kept on feeling its radiance inside me.

Perhaps it was this vibration inside me which guided me that day to find what I needed to know. Like a sleepwalker I kept being drawn to the Asian Art Museum on my daily walk through the park. I had no intention of looking at their special exhibition of Chinese robes, but I walked in anyway and unfailingly arrived at the image of the white hare, a medallion embroidered on the golden robe of a Taoist priest. I was startled. And I was amused. Because here was information about my dream, only a few hours after I had written it down. And when I read the note below, which explained that this medallion represented the moon with "the white hare pounding the elixir of immortality," I was comforted. The comfort reached beyond the images of slaughter in my dream, to the radiance of the white fur. Here was my white hare, that vibrant animal, making the medicine that outlasted death.

But this wasn't the end of gestation for the image within me. It didn't "explain" it. It merely pointed in a possible direction. I continued to carry the dream in me, and the radiance of that white fur kept talking to me. And I kept writing it into my journal, whatever insights came, whatever new images, I wrote them down.

This journey of revelation started with a compelling dream, a dream that terrified me so that I was reluctant to write it down. But what that dream did was sensitize me to pay attention. And what I now know of white radiance, no dream interpretation manual could have taught me. This is the way that seers and poets have always learned, letting the image rise, and listening, letting it teach us.

10 P.M.

Sometimes I take my students out into nature for a day. We go for a walk in the woods or fields, with our journals underarm. This is usually where I teach them about metaphors: I tell them to go and look for a natural metaphor, something in nature that looks at them and becomes a symbolic expression. Next I tell them to go look for a symbolic image of themselves: a plant, an object, an animal, some natural constellation that expresses an inner truth about the person who looks at it. Some of these students have never even heard the word metaphor, and they have certainly never attempted to write poetry. Yet this exercise invariably produces the finest poetry. People go out and realize that all of nature reflects them, that there is metaphor after metaphor waiting to be seen. And they see their images in scarecrows, in barbed-wire fences, in the open valley, in the tree standing at the ridge of the mountain, in the black lambs running to their white mothers, in the embrace of the vine and the tree, in the creek rushing with water: "I am the rock that yearns to move." And the writers come back with all the treasures they found, with their poems disguised as journal entries. And if I tell them that they wrote poems, they often say, no, that couldn't be because they don't like poetry. So I don't tell them for a while. I merely point out to them that they have just found one more way to write in a journal.

And when they have done these first exercises, and gotten all surprised and excited about what nature has in store for them, how it reveals itself and how it reveals us to ourselves, then I send them out for a long walking meditation, with their journals in hand. I tell them to simply walk along slowly and listen to everything: to walk, to notice, to walk on, to listen, to stop once in a while and write, but write very little at a time, to use the journal only to record the revelations that have to be recorded, to notice what really looks at them and to write it down in very few words. And they come back with meditations, having gathered themselves on a level many of them never before conceived of. They come back with a journal full of miracles, a whole basketful of little mirrors of their own consciousness. They come back from their outer journey realizing how profoundly it was also an inner journey. And they look at their journals and see, often for the first time, that their whole writing process is such a journey.

SAN FRANCISCO
MAY 14
SATURDAY, 7 P.M.

Sometimes I like to read to my students from the haiku journals of Basho, the seventeenth-century Japanese poet, who in his life undertook numerous walking meditations, long journeys, and pilgrimages, and whose journal is a weaving of prose and poetry, meditation and travelogue. As poets before him had done for centuries, he traveled to see all the famous places in Japan. He traveled on foot and carried his notebook with him, collecting in this way not only his own impressions of the land but also what came down to him through the centuries, of the consciousness of a culture. When he looked at a tree, he saw the tree in the present time, but also saw the tree that the poet before him had written about, in this very same place. When he wrote a haiku, he also heard the lines which the poets before him had written. And he consciously recorded this process of multiple seeing, and multiple hearing, in his journal, so that for the reader Basho's writing becomes a wonderful collection with information on many levels—the land and its sights, the tradition of writing about it, and the poet's own creative process. We also find out what he ate, where he slept, that he took a bath, who invited him in, who was friendly and who not. For the poet his physical journey, and his written pilgrimage, obviously became the journey of life. For the reader such a notebook becomes a journey of education.

There are of course many other examples from various cultural traditions that could be used to show this. In fact, every diary is to some extent a gathering basket of a culture at the same time that it is a record of individual consciousness. Every journal is a process of education, for the writer and for the reader. In Basho's book it is clearly visible that this process has to do with walking. The journal is a process of education through movement, in the physical and metaphorical sense.

Very few students today have any idea how one received an education before the invention of public transportation, and before the printing press produced books for the masses. You walked! And you had a notebook, a sort of journal, and you took notes of what you saw and heard. Artists walked with their sketchbooks to Rome or Florence. And students walked to Paris or Milan or Prague to hear a learned man read from his notebook, his journal of sorts. And whatever you managed to collect through this process of traveling and listening and note taking, that was your education. You came home with your notebook under your arm, and that was your book of learning. All that you learned on the journey out, and all that you learned on the journey back home, was your education. Those who were well off rode a horse or took a carriage, everyone else walked. But in any case it was a quest that involved a day's stretch of time, a day's travel, a day's experience. And the book that recorded such a daily process became a jour-nal or a dia-ry.

Notebooks that record the daily experience through time were of course kept not just by students, or scholars, or artists, who traveled on the road of education, but by many other travelers on the road of life. Columbus kept a journal on his voyage out into the unknown ocean. Darwin kept a journal on his travels to South America, and his detailed daily observations became the basis for his theory of evolution. Many a mother has kept a diary of the growth of her child, or kept anxious notes about the course of a sickness. In each of these cases the notebook was there to record a journey into the unknown. It is a record of the daily experience through time, of the daily steps toward a larger understand-ing. And in each case the writer assumed that by recording daily portions of his or her experience, the larger nature of the journey—of the earth, of life, of illness—would become visible.

Whether such a notebook is called a jour-nal or a dia-ry varies throughout history and seems to depend on what word was more fashionable in English at the time. Sometimes I come across serious articles discussing the difference between a journal and a diary. The first part of both words mean "day," one from French, the other from Latin. Some people argue that a "diary" is more intimate than a "journal," but I have read notebooks by scientists who called them diaries, and notebooks by lovers who called them journals, so I think it is useless to make definitions. At the present time in America a "diary" is often thought of as the intimate notebook of a teenager, while almost everyone else seems to write in a "journal." I use the word "journal" because it is the standard term used today. It makes little difference what you call the notebook, or whether the content is personal or not. This is a particular form of writing that has to do with recording a journey, inner or outer, and the recording is done in daily fragments. This form of writing has to do with writing down a process, a movement through time, but writing it down in small steps. Some journal writers like to take their notebooks on a physical walk, others move through a landscape of metaphor, but all record the journey of life.

Journal writing and walking have been linked together by many a writer. Henry David Thoreau, a great journal writer and a passionate walker, wrote a wonderful essay called "Walking." What he says in that essay has much to do with

the walk of life, and especially with the creative process—
what it means to move about freely according to the needs
of the moment. Most of what he says about walking can also
be applied to writing:

> They who never go to the Holy Land in their walks . . . are
> mere idlers and vagabonds; but they who go there are
> saunterers in the good sense, such as I mean. . . . For this
> is the secret of successful sauntering. He who sits still in a
> house all the time may be the greatest vagrant of all; but the
> saunterer, in the good sense, is no more vagrant than the
> meandering river, which is all the while sedulously seeking
> the shortest course to the sea.

Thoreau's own journals are walking meditations, and as in
Basho's journals, there is a collection process going on. He
gathers the land, he gathers himself, and he gathers his
understanding of civilization and of wilderness. And each
time he walks in his landscape, each time he writes in his
notebook, new revelations are recorded. And we, the readers of his journals, are privileged to watch this wonderful
saunterer, this meandering river, find his path.

SAN FRANCISCO
MAY 15
SUNDAY, 5 P.M.

When I was a small child, we had a picture book that I liked
very much. It was about a little boy who walked into the
woods with a basket in his hand to gather berries for his
mother. But he couldn't find any berries at all and so sat
down on a tree stump and cried. At that moment something
touched him, and he looked down and saw a blueberry
dwarf, and the dwarf invited the boy to come and play in the
woods. As soon as he agreed to this, the dwarf touched him
again, and the boy became very small. But he didn't know
that. The way he experienced it was that everything around
him became very large and very alive—mice became horses,
leaves became sailboats—and they had a wonderful day in the
woods. They visited the blueberry people and the lingon-
berry people, and in the evening the boy found himself sitting
on a tree stump, rubbing his eyes, and his baskets were full
of berries, but he wasn't sure how all this had come about.

The process of gathering ourselves is a mysterious one.
Sometimes we are not sure how it has come about. One
morning we rub our eyes and the baskets are full, and we are
not sure how it happened. I open my journal and find that I
have already been in that place in the woods. My own words
of wisdom are on the page, and I didn't even know about it.
Going into the woods with too much purpose isn't very
helpful, the baskets often stay empty that way. But agreeing
to play, making lengthy detours, becoming small so that

77

everything else can become large, all that can be very helpful for writing. We need to get lost in the creative process for some time, in order to find ourselves. Sometimes we need to lose the memory of previous journal entries in order to find this one. We are multilimbed and strange creatures. If the path is too straight, we distort ourselves. We gather ourselves little by little, and with the help of mysterious forces. It is good not to question all the time how it all hangs together. It is good to gather one berry after another and to sail down the river on a fragile leaf, all at the same time, finding that your basket is already standing at the shore, filling itself.

SAN FRANCISCO
MAY 16
MONDAY, EVENING

A vision:

This morning, as I was doing a breathing meditation, a strange and beautiful vision appeared in my body. First shadows appeared behind my third eye, fleeting shadows, as if blown by wind, and more shadows in the throat. But when I came to the heart, it became apparent that I was like a sun, a center for rays going out every-where. And when I breathed in, I returned the light to myself, and it appeared that I was dark—all those rays, all those limbs, like a sea anemone pulling in, and as if the light flickered and withdrew.

And when I breathed out again, then the light came up as if from the center, but also as if from the underside of all those anemone limbs, and it radiated intensely outward. And again, breathing in—softly folding my dark anemone rays, breathing out—unfolding and radiating light out to the tip of each limb and beyond. It was like a slow peaceful pulse. I knew now what light and dark were, and how the universe breathed.

LATER

Yesterday I called my mother in Europe, to tell her that I wasn't going to be here for a while, that I was going to Oregon to take a workshop, and that she wouldn't be able to reach me. And then my father came to the phone! My father came to the phone and wanted to talk to me! A gentle, ordinary conversation. He seemed better somehow and more content. Mysterious ways of the universe.

Apparently the whole family was there. Both of my sisters came to the phone and talked. And my little niece, age thirteen, came to tell me that she wants to come to America to visit me. Could she come this summer?

RED BLUFF
MAY 20
FRIDAY, 10 P.M.

Today I began my journey north. Such excitement packing
the car, leaving the city, driving over the coastal hills, away
from the fog of the Pacific, and dipping down into the hot air
of the central valley—ah, summer. Heat, ripe grain fields,
the smell of hay, and the rice fields! I have never before
noticed the sky reflected in a green field—the lightest green,
a mass of shoots pushing up through the water, the blue sky
between them, and occasionally a white heron, standing in
the field and sky at once.

I have driven this route many times before but never tire
of it. Perhaps because there are no big cities, only the drone
of the freeway, and the hot souplike air with all the smells
of the plants, thick with the scent of growth, and this freeway
artery carrying us on urgently over the body of the earth, her
blond hills undulating by. From two hundred miles south one
can see Mount Shasta standing in front, the road constantly
pointing toward it, and the entire freeway with its cars and
trucks rushing north as if on some wild pilgrimage. And
the mountain stands, and we never seem to get closer, mile
after mile.

ASHLAND

MAY 21

SATURDAY, 8 P.M.

At three o'clock in the morning I woke up in my motel room
in Red Bluff. There was a sharp peeping sound: a single
intense peep and then nothing for about two minutes, and
then another sharp peep. This continued and the sound was
so intense and so short that I could not locate it. First I
suspected my new alarm clock. I took the battery out, but
the peep sound was still in the room. I looked the whole
room over but could not find anything. Perhaps a bird outside the window? I have occasionally heard a hummingbird
make a very sharp short sound like that. But at three in the
morning and this consistently? Perhaps the smoke alarm? I
couldn't tell. And by this time I had decided it didn't matter
what it was. Obviously I could not sleep. Perhaps something
was trying to warn me, or simply tell me to get up now and
start driving.

By the time I was dressed the sound was gone. I was not
surprised about that. I began to drive with the first signs of
dawn, and as I moved along the road, I thought that if I were
a fiction writer I could probably make something out of this.
I would experience the beginning of the tale, this strange
warning in the morning, and then I would "make up" a story
out of that. But I am a journal writer, and so my stories come
slowly, installment by installment, as they come to me on my
path, as I live them, as I receive them, as they reveal themselves to me. There may be no story to tell from this inci-

dent, or there may be, but it could take ten years to reveal itself.

I love the stories that grow in the journal, as I love the story that grows in life. You never have any idea what will be next. You just keep your eyes and ears open for all the signs from the universe and let it grow. You don't worry about plot, you don't force the next chapter. Most stories stay fragments forever. You only know part of the whole, but you collect each pebble, each installment, for its own beauty, not worrying whether they will fit together later on.

As I moved along the road in early dawn, I realized how magnificent dawn is, how rarely we see it all the way from its dark beginning to its radiant sunrise. How rarely we arise to see this part of the day, unless something rudely wakes us up and sends us on our way. I thought of the many stories that get written, how bored I often get reading them, because they move over and over along predictable patterns of fiction, never bothering to get up in the dark and observe what the world reveals, always pushing the story to some urgent conclusion, or foreshadowing everything right from the first page on.

What then did those eerie peeps this morning foreshadow for me? Nothing for that day. I was privileged to see a magnificent sunrise. I saw the volcano stand alone in rose-colored light, rising to fourteen thousand feet, and we below still in darkness. I was alone on the road to see it. And I was grateful to have been wakened. I greeted the mountain and said my thanks to the peep. And that is my story, or a

fragment of it. Perhaps every journal entry is the story of
one's awakening.

ASHLAND
MAY 26
THURSDAY, 7:20 P.M.

Writing in the rain. Risking it, sitting out here under the
trees at my picnic table in front of my cabin. Is it going
to come through? Now a drop, and now another one. But
the tree above is thick, I sit under an umbrella of green,
and the birds love this gentle shower before dusk. And I love
to sit here, writing away between raindrops. The page
will be wet. I see it coming. But I will not let that hinder
me. A wet journal, a wet walk. Bird symphonies before the
evening.

I have been here for several days now, participating in a
workshop on human energy systems. How much I enjoy
being the student for a change, instead of being the teacher.
Being a student, absorbing and absorbing, and taking notes.
Really, I am always the student, all my life, taking notes in
my journal on all the lessons that come along. Asking huge
questions into this white and patient and divine ear. And
finding the answers hundreds of pages later, written in my
own hand. "What is health?" someone in class asked today,

and I couldn't help but think of my writing, and I thought: The flow, the flow, always the flow.

SAN FRANCISCO
MAY 31
TUESDAY, AFTERNOON

On the morning I left Ashland, the man came out from the cabin next door and brought me a puppet. I loved it at first sight. The arms are spread out in a fierce shamanic dance, and the head is a duck face. It's the eagle dancer and the fool in one. He looks ominous in his black smock, but I want to embrace him.

So the puppet and I went on our way, drove southeast, out to the arid high country of northeastern California. There we got out of the car and went for a long walk among juniper trees and lava flows, a silent landscape with nothing but the wind, and the movement of the earth arrested for the time being. We listened for a long time to these ancient rocks that had come liquid out of the belly of the earth, had cooled and taken on form, merely waiting for the next movement in their cycle through the elements—from fire, to earth, to water, to air. I realized I was looking at the journal of the earth and felt awe for its grandness, its majestic entries page after page. Next to me an old juniper tree was probing its roots down into volcanic rock, down into the chapter of its own nourishment. I stood there in gratitude, being able to read all this.

And the puppet and I did a little dance. We stood on a big rock and sang a song, and the sun touched us, as it has touched the earth for eons. And I wondered what other great journals were written in the universe and came to us, letter by letter, on those warm rays, those brilliant frequencies.

And the puppet suggested to me that I drive west and visit an old Indian man who lives at the bottom of Mount Shasta. I decided that was a good idea, drove through the late afternoon, and arrived dusty at a trailer park where I had never been before. The old man invited me in. I had met him several times before at sweat lodge ceremonies but had never visited him. We sat and talked. Mostly I listened while he told stories: how he came to the mountain, how he had been called to come, and how the mountain talked to him, gave him instructions about the work that needed to be done in this world. I listened until the sun went down, and I thought—if we could only read the journals of the earth, if we would only listen to her, page after page, we would all know what to do, what our work was. I wished I could read her better, this mother of ours. I wished I had been taught, my ears and my eyes, to recognize all her creatures.

When I left, the old man told me that he was going into the wilderness for a while, at the end of June, with a small group of people. He invited me to come along. My thoughts went racing through my calendar, my schedules, all the work I had to do. But my mouth was already open and said, "Yes, I would love to come."

When I got back to my car, the puppet took one quick look at me and said, "Now you are really in for a journey!" And he seemed to grin all over his black duck face.

On second thought, I decided to show the old man one more thing. Digging around in my car, I reached for the large rock I had found by the side of the road. It had markings that looked exactly like ancient pictographs. I went back to the trailer and showed him the rock. He touched it quickly with both hands as if to read it and said, "Where did you find this rock?" I told him, "By the side of the road." And he said, "Well, then you better read it since it came to you." I drove home that night, back to the cities, hundreds of miles, thinking that I carried the journal of the earth with me.

San Francisco
June 8
Wednesday, morning

Clouds in the sky, the sun very bright in between. A man reads a poem on the radio. He sees a white rabbit in the desert and calls it: daylight moon.

≋

I see a rainbow in the sky. The weather is strange this year. Clouds in the dry season, puffy white clouds sweeping across a drought landscape: brilliant water conception.

≋

I see a rainbow. The white light of the sky becomes the aura of the earth. I remember the teacher who read his students' energy fields and said: "I don't need to read your journals, you radiate everything, your auras are all around you."

≋

John Muir walked in the mountains of California, wrote about the subtle colors he saw in Yosemite and he thought that the Sierra Nevada should be called: the range of light.

SAN FRANCISCO
JUNE 13
MONDAY, 4 P.M.

I have been asking myself what strange times these are. Everything seems to be on hold and yet yearning terribly to be released at the same time. Sometimes I hold my breath as if trying to help someone else in labor, until I realize it must be my own labor, and the point is not to hold one's breath in any case, but to breathe and breathe, to exhale and inhale, to contract and expand with the rhythm of the universe, no matter what is in preparation.

Yesterday we had an earthquake in San Francisco, not devastating, but my little house shook, and I shook and ran to the door frame, trying to breathe deeply. Then it stopped, and I sat down at my desk. But I noticed then that for the brief moment that I stood and shook with the house, I had been in the rhythm of something so often forgotten. Some people would perhaps call it fear—a fast heartbeat, an intense alertness, hearing, noticing everything. But I would say it is a moment of intense aliveness, of instant recognition of our deep pulse. A moment of remembering the energy of the thunderbolt and that it is in us all the time, and that we must not forget. Indeed, that we constantly yearn for it, this intense aliveness, but that we mostly put it on hold for later, until some terrible event, or the earth itself, shakes us and we realize why we are here.

Joseph Campbell said yesterday on a television program that people always think they are looking for "the meaning of life," but that he doesn't think so. He said, "I don't think we are looking for meaning. I think we are looking for the experience of being alive." How right he is. No one in the middle of an earthquake wants to know the meaning of life, you just want to keep on breathing and doing and being all the wonderful things that life is. And for the split second after you know that you are safe, you ask yourself why you have not done it, this intense deep living, why you are always just thinking about it, saving it for later. There are people who remember these moments of danger as euphoric moments, because they know no other way of being so deeply alive.

Which brings me back to writing. When people come to my writing classes, I often ask them why they are here. And they will invariably come up with a story about how they have "always wanted to write, but . . ." It doesn't really matter whether it is a sixty-five-year-old man who has "always wanted to write but . . ." waited until retirement, or whether it is a college-age student who has put it off for the last few years because she was afraid she wasn't good enough, or any of the many other variations of this situation. The point is that they all delayed it. And that they needed to go to an officially approved class in order to give themselves permission. And that they need to hear over and over from their teacher that what they are doing is fine, and that they are wonderful writers. And what many of them are here for, and really want to know from me, is: Do they have talent, and are they going to make it? And when I tell them that all of this has nothing to do with being deeply alive, they do not understand what I mean at all.

When I first began writing in my little notebooks, I didn't even know that there were such things as writing classes, or that there were people authorized to tell other people whether they have talent or not. I was terribly worried that someone would find my notebooks, that people would ridicule me or think I was crazy, but this didn't stop me from scribbling on. What I did know was that there was a delicious sense of euphoria anytime I did anything I really wanted to do, whether it was scribbling in my notebook, or painting

Mother's kitchen closet with bright colors the weekend she was away, or jumping from the roof of our woodshed onto the neighbor's pigsty, or simply rolling on the bare ground when the snow finally left.

It doesn't have to do with danger, or with talent, or with finding out if you can make it in the approved way. It has to do with being alive, with seeing the beauty of something in this very moment and not postponing it, not thinking about it, not waiting until retirement, but to ride on that thunder-bolt of the moment and feel that it is real. This is what all of us really want. And this is why I am writing. It makes me feel intensely alive. Perhaps not as critically as in the middle of an earthquake, but close enough to keep hearing the deep pulse of the universe and feel that it is here with me now, and now, and now, and comes out of my mouth with every breath, and out of my fingers—every word a little pulse.

How can we ask someone's permission to do that? Is there anyone authorized to tell us that we have sufficient talent to be deeply alive? It is absurd, this preoccupation with success and the fear of failure, which causes people to delay living. Do I need a grade to tell me that I created a real poem? There are pages and pages of my writing, volumes of journals and many other texts, that from the standpoint of publishing will never make it, or in retrospect turn out to be simply not very good. But the sense of pleasure and aliveness they gave me while writing them, is their true value, and that can never be estimated by anyone else.

This morning I turned on the radio while fixing my breakfast, and a man who taught the piano was being interviewed. I never really found out who he was, but it didn't matter. After a few minutes I turned the conversation off because I had all the information I needed.

The man was an enthusiastic musician, one could hear that. He was saying that the way to teach people how to play an instrument is to teach them to be playful with it. To have fun, to be excited with it. To be silly and serious all at once, but at any rate to be very active with it. He was saying that students always came to him, so terribly concerned about proper technique—how the fingers must be held, how one must sit correctly. And he quoted examples of famous pianists who invariably broke all the conventional rules but who were passionately involved with their instruments. They were passionately alive through music.

I stood in the kitchen smiling. I had just written, yesterday, the pages about being deeply alive through writing, and I loved the fact that someone else had gotten up early in the morning in order to demonstrate the same point. The point being that any form or technique one can teach to a student is only helpful if the student is already vibrating with the spirit of the craft. And the most helpful thing one can do for a student in this time of ours, which is so focused on technique and success and results that we are all suffocating from it, is to give him or her permission to be truly alive—whether through music, or writing, or any other means.

But the interviewer wasn't really very happy with this. He kept saying how wonderful it was to make people so excited about playing the piano, and this was fine for amateurs. But what about professionals? What about real concert pianists? Wasn't that a different story altogether—here technique was what really counted!

I could tell that he had not heard anything. He could not let go, kept coming back to it over and over. And the piano teacher was silent for a minute, perhaps he needed to take a deep breath. And then he began from the beginning—how people didn't know what music was, what art really was. And I turned off the radio and wished him luck with his explanation, and was grateful that we had heard each other, so early in the morning.

AFTERNOON

When people come to a writing class, they often come with considerable pain. Certainly this is how most of us start. Life hurts so terribly, and it can't really be said to anyone, and so we begin to scribble on white paper, or to fiddle with the ivory keys of the piano, or we move a dark brush over a white canvas, or any of the other means by which we whisper ourselves into the divine ear. It starts perhaps out of a deep yearning for someone to listen. But it is also an attempt to find a form which holds the reality of live experience, in all its terror and its joy, and its inexplicable ways.

But the problem is that most people don't know that is what they are trying to do. Or they are in such agony that they are unable to see anything except their own pain, and their writing simply becomes a scream for recognition of their suffering. I have been in such places of pain, so I say this with great compassion and respect. But how is that recognition to be brought about? This is the question many people focus on, and as far as I am concerned, it is the wrong question. It is the question that naturally comes up when you are desperate, when you are forced to live a false life, and when you live in an environment which is completely focused on visible results and public success.

In such a situation it is common to assume that there are certain steps to be taken, certain techniques to be learned, in order to achieve the recognition that is so wanted. And it is also natural to be very afraid of failure, so afraid, in fact, that you are willing to deny yourself the need to write at all, or that your entire focus is on learning it "the right way." At which point the need to be intensely alive, and the desire to express the reality of this aliveness, become completely over-shadowed by the need to be approved of and the need to succeed. People think that if only they could be published, if only they could become famous, and well known, and listened to, then their pain would stop, then they could start living real lives, then they would know that their art is good.

Obviously all of us want a certain amount of recognition in our lives from the people around us. And a writer has to know if he/she is reaching anyone with his/her writing, if the texts are somehow real for others, if anyone out there is responding to them. We all need some validation for our work. But the point is that the excitement and satisfaction must come primarily from the process itself, not from the results. And when the excitement comes from the process, then one learns more about the real work of writing than if one is completely focused on certain results.

Perhaps I like the journal so much because it is such a modest form. It is not the great novel. It is a rather quiet and private form, but it allows me to express my pain and my pleasure, my thoughts and my visions. It lets me be real, to be alive through writing, without succeeding or failing at it, without approval or disapproval. It allows me to document my life journey, so I can look at it later, and get a glimpse of what it might be. And in the end, through years of journal writing, I have learned much about writing, about technique and craft and language, and about myself—what I see, and what I don't see. And about the spirit of things—when it is in me and when not. And what a text looks like when it is alive, and when it is dead.

EVENING

My first role as a writing teacher is often to be a nurse, to calm the fears of students, to assure them that it is all right to write about anything and that I am not here to sentence them to death. Each time I walk into a new class I am amazed at the fear level. How did we manage to put people into such terror about writing? In most classes it takes weeks to establish a level of trust so that the real work can then be done.

And sometimes no amount of gentle assurance is good enough to change their conviction that we are here to determine who is going to make it and who is not.

My next role is to get them very excited about writing. This isn't possible as long as they are terribly afraid. This role has much to do with taboo-breaking, with all the imagined rules that people have in their heads and that keep them from writing: I can't talk about this, and can't talk about that. And this is not interesting, and that is silly. And I must make complete sentences. And everything must have a beginning, a middle, and an end. Endless rules, drilled into us from grammar school on. It is hard to get excited about writing, when ninety percent of what comes to mind is not good enough, or not right somehow.

Once the real work of writing is somewhat on its way, my role as a teacher shifts again. In this role I am not a nurse who reassures people, and I am not a clown who jumps over all the false barriers. I have to show people how they falsify themselves and their texts. This has much to do with craft but also with the spirit of a text. Learning to recognize cliché statements, overused phrases, worn-out standard movie scenes, and lots of other dead material that we substitute when we don't honor the live thing, has much to do with craft, but mostly it has to do with learning to recognize the truth of an experience. It has to do with craft because it deals with understanding how a text works within a cultural tradition. But it has to do with one's own spirit because it involves sensing if this particular expression is true for me at this moment in time. Many students are unable to recognize this live spirit in themselves and in their writing. Others are perfectly willing to sacrifice it in exchange for a text that will more likely please someone and "succeed," as they imagine success.

Sometimes when I comment on a text, the student will say to me, "Yes, but if I really wrote that way, no one would ever publish it." And I might say, "That may or may not be true. But at any rate you can write it into your journal. The divine ear can take in everything. And the act of actually writing it down, without focusing on the success of it, might also bring something alive in you. It might make it possible for you to see how to put something into the world, as it is, in its own truth, and without falsifying it, born fully alive, out of yourself."

San Francisco
June 16
Thursday, morning

Dream:
I am standing in a garden, and next to it is a field of maize. Between the corn, beans have been planted and are climbing up the cornstalks.

There are people, they want to harvest the field. But it is not ripe yet! I am shocked. I try to talk to them: Please don't do that. It will only be a little while, and the corn will be ripe! But they answer

carelessly: It doesn't matter, there is a drought condition, no time
to wait, the beans are ripe, and that's good enough.

I can't believe it. I look at the tall maize, an entire standing field,
fully green. And they want to rip it out. It would have ripened in
its own time!

I see the hands reaching for the stalks. Then suddenly the wind
rustles through, as if the field were dry.

SAN FRANCISCO
JUNE 17
FRIDAY, NOON

I want to talk about stories. Stories that ripen in their own
time, and stories that come to us fully finished except we
don't recognize it, and all the material that's ripe for the
picking anytime we open our eyes and ears. And stories that
come like a gift, like an act of completion, many years after
we have stopped looking for them.

A story in a journal is not like a short story. It doesn't
necessarily have a beginning, a middle, and an end, and it
isn't usually written with intention. And that is the beauty of
it. It grows before we know it, out of life, out of our process.
And it is not hindered by our intentions—all the things we
think have to be in it, what a story is supposed to look like.

97

Students often come to a writing class and announce that they have an "idea" for a story. It's often an idea they have had for a long time, sometimes for years. And one day they were going to write about it, as soon as they gave themselves permission to write at all, and as soon as they made sure that this "idea" was a good one. They ask me what I think of it. Then I sometimes tell them that an idea doesn't make a text. A story that is figured out in one's head beforehand is, in my experience, rarely a very exciting one. And what most writers actually experience is that they perhaps start with some idea, but then the story writes itself, moves into directions unexpected, and in general seems to have its very own will.

The most helpful thing one can teach anyone in terms of writing material is that this material can be found anywhere at any time. You don't need to have an idea, and it isn't a matter of finding the right one. It is a matter of seeing what's under your nose and making something of it. People spend endless and agonizing hours trying to "think of something to write." This is useless. When one goes for a walk, one doesn't "try to think of something to see." One simply starts walking and opens one's eyes. Of course there are people who try to plan a walk ahead of time, and plan what they will experience on the walk. And in that case they probably experience very little. Some people travel this way too. They make an exact outline of all they want to see and expect it to be just as it is in the travel brochure. When you live life this way, all you are doing is matching expectations to results. You are not making a journey into the unknown. The most exciting journeys I have, in life as in art, are those when

I take whatever I see as a revelation. And that is also how I write.

I often like to place myself in situations where I don't have any idea what I am going to do next, and I love to watch my creative process unfold at such times. I love to spend time without a plan and simply respond to what occurs in the moment. When it comes to writing, I learned that if you trust the present moment and open yourself to it, then what needs to be there will be there, and what needs to be said will be said. And it doesn't matter what you pick as a first sentence, or what outside stimulation or inside memory you start with, you will eventually get around to writing what has been waiting inside you to be written.

The situation of writing from an open moment can be applied to any writing, not just private journal writing. But it works especially well for the journal, because that is where we often involuntarily document the mystical journeys we didn't know we were taking. It works well for writing the stories we didn't know were inside us. Much of this entire manuscript is being written this way, as a walk into the unknown, as a sequence of insights about writing. I did not have an outline. I simply sat down one day and began, as I would begin any journal. Occasionally I think about what I want to say in one of the next entries, but when I actually sit down, I create a quiet empty space, a small moment of meditation, and then I start with what suggests itself. Sometimes the first sentence is there, sometimes an image is there. Occasionally the radio delivers a seemingly incidental message and I make use of it, or I look out the window and see what messengers the universe sends. When writing this way, you simply begin and trust that today's entry will write itself, that some inner master already knows how it will fit into the network of your whole creative journey, in a much more beautiful way than you could ever have planned with an outline.

When you write in a journal with this sort of trust, and when you do it for a long time, then "stories" begin to develop that one could not have conceived of in a deliberate way. As long as one is very purposeful and sits down with ideas already formed, or has in mind what one must write about today, this does not tend to happen. The reason many people get so bored with journal writing is that they enslave themselves. They think they "have to report" to the journal what they did the previous day. But the journal doesn't care. In fact, it would love to be liberated from this boring lesson plan and participate in the creative flow of the present moment. When this happens, then the true stories begin to surface. By this I mean a network of meaning that grows slowly, and that narrates something with a visible thread through many fragments of texts. I mean the journeys and deeper themes we are working on without knowing it.

Many kinds of stories grow in a journal. There are of course the stories of one's actions, and if you look at these actions over several months, they might tell a larger tale. A series of metaphors that one uses might become a theme after a while, and thus paint a larger canvas. The same can be true for dream images and recurring dream patterns. Dreams often come in sequences, and such a sequence can narrate a deeper life process. Memories that keep surfacing, images that keep suggesting themselves, what one tends to see and report about, and what not, all make a story. I live in a city environment, but what I mostly notice and write down are things from nature, and I suppose that tells something about me. But I do not mean ''story'' here in terms of just a psychological pattern that evolves about the journal writer. I mean a larger pattern of consciousness, the cycles of one's being.

And when we become conscious of these larger dimensions of our life, how they surface through many texts that were not planned or designed, then we become even more trusting of our own writing. We can see a story in its complete wholeness, or we can recognize what is not ripe yet and needs its own time to unfold.

SAN FRANCISCO
JUNE 19
SUNDAY, AFTERNOON

This weekend I drove out into the country, to the little redwood house where I used to live years ago. Other people live there now, but I go to visit once in a while. This time I stayed overnight. The people had to go somewhere, so I had my old house to myself. This house where so much of my real writing began, where my journals blossomed, where dreams and visions came. This house where the outside and the inside became one great mythical landscape, where there were no borders between the land, and my garden, and my house, and myself. This place where I lived in sacred time, where daily life stretched into one mysterious journey after another. This place which I had to leave because it became too expensive, because a freeway was built in the little town nearby, and many houses. Because people came by the thousands, and because you cannot live in sacred landscape when the land is called property.

And so I slept in my old house and woke up to a beautiful morning. I walked on the horse mountain, early, walked along the horse path in the gentle sunny air. A red-tailed hawk flew up in front of me. I went to the little hill that looks like the shoulder of a child. It was all so long ago, but I didn't feel nostalgia this time, just peace. Up on the hill the horses were snorting around in the brush. And as I got up there, where my old mother oak stood, the tree where I had gone so often with my pain and my sorrow, there under the oak stood the white horse, calmly feeding.

I stopped and prayed a little, such a beautiful moment. As if something that years ago would not come together, now calmly did. The white horse moved over a bit, and I sat down. Was it the same horse, was it another? This horse which had always evaded me when I lived here. I would see her from my window when I sat in the house writing, would see her up on the hill, but I could never find her when I went walking. Perhaps I was afraid of finding her. I don't know.

Now she stood a little farther over, nibbling, and looking

at me from time to time. Then she dragged her tail over a bush, as if to leave me some of her magic hair. I later went over and found one long white hair and took it. The white horse moved down the hill, turning back from time to time, peeking at me from behind tree trunks as I held her hair in my hand. I had the feeling she had healed me, and I would never be afraid of an animal again that came to help me. I walked down the hill to the house, and sat on the porch, and remembered the many poems I had written about her. Or was it about another white horse, way back in my childhood, in another time, another house, another mountain? Or were those horses all blending now, and she knew that as she looked at me gently this time?

I spent the morning sitting on the porch, just me and the cats, on my green grapevined porch, reading and dreaming. And gradually as I sat there, I became aware of the past that lived there. Not just my solitary past with plant and animal helpers, but the many people who had visited. There was my brother, on a winter visit from Europe, sitting on the railing, laughing, and tanning his body in the California sun. His body whole, and he laughing. And another year there was my mother in a rocking chair, looking out at the garden, holding my black cat Sheba. My ex-husband was there, with his new wife. And my friends and neighbors, their children tumbling down the stairs. There was my aunt painting a new canvas under the persimmon tree, and my uncle swinging in the hammock between the redwoods. I always thought of myself as alone in that place, but many had come for a visit.

But pain had come to visit too. I saw myself as I sat on that porch year after year, journal in hand, trying to put two continents together, fusing in the form of metaphors what could not be done in physical reality. Healing the wounds of transplantation from one culture to another, from one language to another. Desperately trying to make one family out of the different people I loved and who were so far apart. How many letters written here? How many journal entries, until I realized that I was trying to put myself together, a large unknown shape, out of many broken pieces. Was trying to put myself together, my world together—through writing.

And so I sat there yesterday, on the porch of my old house, for a long time, until I realized it was not my house anymore. It was gone, that time, those people. My brother is gone! The friends who used to live around there have moved in all directions. But mostly that time in my life was gone. That was not my house! It *was* someone else's furniture! I have a different shape now. I know my shape now.

I sat there breathing in and out, letting it go. That past, the life there, letting it go—feeling so strongly that something new was coming in but not at that place. I no longer belonged to that house! I gently closed the door behind me and left. It was late afternoon, and the time near sunset. I drove home through orange-purple light and knew that sacred time lived inside me. That's where I belong, no matter where I live.

SAN FRANCISCO
JUNE 21
TUESDAY, MORNING
SUMMER SOLSTICE

On a sunny morning, on summer solstice, one ought to go out into the world, walk between earth and sky, and smile at the sun for its brilliant radiance through the year. And consider all the way stations that we call days and months, and how we are affected when the earth rests in those places. This is the journey of our energy, of our growth, the cycle from light into darkness and into light again.

In the mountains where I grew up as a small child, people lit fires on the night of summer solstice. They would light them at dusk, as soon as the daylight faded, and we children would go out and wait for the first fire to appear, way up on some high mountain peak. And we would call to our parents, "There it is, there it is, the first one!" And the dark mountains would light up with hundreds of flickering lights, little stars, little suns, signaling into the night sky on some high mountain ridge. And as a small child I understood. There was safety in that magic, and I felt at home in it. I always thought that when I grew up I would carry one of those fires into the mountains.

I never did carry the light into those mountains. But there are many kinds of paths to be walked, and many fires to be carried. I light my bonfires on pure white paper. I whisper the little suns into the divine ear—the patient one that receives our fires in the dark night. I walk in my journal, and that, too, is a walk between heaven and earth, that, too, is a cycle of the light.

SAN FRANCISCO
JULY 6
WEDNESDAY, NOON

When one returns from a journey in the wilderness, one doesn't know what to say. Perhaps it is a matter of language, the language that spoke to us in that place of the woods. The language of bears and of high mountain lakes, of cedar and rock, of salmon swimming upstream. The language that once was ours but that now needs translation.

I sit here at my city window with the cars going by, and I think of how to translate the language of bears—that soft paw print in the dust, with the veins showing, and the pulse of life still hovering where he passed minutes before me on the path. The language of my body as it translates his presence—my ears hearing, my nose sniffing, my heart respecting his being.

When one returns from the wilderness, one seems to carry light. There is a clarity in everything except words, and the task of translation seems burdensome. For seven days I walked in the Marble Mountains of northern California. I walked with a small group of people and the old Indian man who was our teacher. I carried a notebook with me, a small journal in my backpack, but when I opened it up, there was nothing in it but bear tracks, bird droppings, sweet plant whispers, the roots crawling through.

On the last day of my journey I sat by a river with long green hair. It was like the hair of some wild river woman, swirling at my feet, as if she wanted to caress me. And the river woman whispered to me, she said, "Put your feet in the water, put your hands in." And as soon as I did I saw the fish. Hundreds of salmon, swimming upstream, swimming straight into the fierce rapids of the river. And the green hair caressed my feet, and I forgot about time. And when I finally turned to go, I saw that my backpack had fallen into the water, as if the wild woman wanted to claim it, as if she wanted to claim my journal and make the task of translation impossible. And as if she wanted to say, "Everyone has to come for himself, there is no translation, there is only a return to the source. And whoever returns will know the language of the wilderness, and whoever looks into the waters of Spirit Lake will know his own face."

And yet I want to try it, this difficult task of voicing. Perhaps I need it, perhaps we all need it, this translation from the language of the source, this labor of love, where we all try to reach one another, each with our own strange words. Perhaps I need to translate myself to myself, and maybe that is what the journal has always done for me.

Journal of the Journey to the Source

First on the morning of the first day I swam at dawn, and the river otter came and swam with me in the pools of the Scott River. We hiked all day. In the evening of the first day we swam in Sky High Lake, and the osprey fell from the sky at sunset, scooping up fish, and diving back up into light.

≈

On the morning of the second day the old man fried fresh trout for everyone. It multiplied. First there were five fish, then another, then more. Enough for everyone. We hiked over Marble Mountain ridge, wading through wildflowers. I picked sweet mountain sage, an eagle appeared. In the evening we camped at Spirit Lake. A strange bird kept calling. We never saw it, but it kept calling from the unknown. At dusk mists formed on the lake and danced slow circles over the water. The old man said, "This is Spirit Lake!" And I heard him.

≈

On the third day we built a sweat lodge. I have never seen sunlight so sweet, as it broke in between fir trees at noon to light up the earth, and the lodge poles, and our hands, golden, as we worked. So quiet it was, so blessed. On the night of the third day I sat up in my sleeping bag and listened to the old man singing far away in the woods. I wanted to sing back to him but did not know if this was right. In the morning he told me he was honoring his dream—he was dancing, in the night, to honor his dream. Then I knew what was right—for me, for all of us—to honor what comes to us, anywhere, and at any time of day.

≈

I cannot write what happened on the fourth day because it is too deep in my chest. That day I listened to a rock. And my face was in it.

≋

And I will not tell what happened on the fifth or the sixth day, because it does not matter. We learned to respect each other, and ourselves, and all that surrounds us. I didn't know about the incredible softness of a bear's paw as it imprints into dust. I didn't know that deer will stand still if you sing to them.

≋

On the evening of the seventh day I sat by the rushing rapids of Ishi Pishi. I sat in the last sunlight of the day, my feet dangling in the swirling hair of the green river woman. And just a little farther over, where the current was rushing wildly over the rocks, a large salmon stood perfectly still, facing into the current. I realized it wasn't standing still at all, it was using every bit of energy it had to swim straight into the current. And I thought: What would happen if we humans did this? If we swam straight into the rushing currents of the divine, without doubt or hesitation, swam straight into the rapids of this life force, letting the sacred rush through us, and vibrating with it?

≋

On the evening of the last day all my papers fell into the river. And I fished them out. It didn't matter. Now the river was on the page. Earlier that day, when saying good-bye, the old man had smiled at me, and had said: "Now you tell your story, but tell it with your eyes, and with your ears, and with your skin." And here I was, with my eyes and my skin in the salmon, and my words in the river.

I want to talk about movement, and rhythm. The rhythm of our life, the rhythm of breathing, of our actions, and the rhythm of writing which is merely a reflection of all these movements. People often complain to me that they cannot write, that they have writer's block. It is so fashionable to talk about "writer's block," as if this were some mysterious virus, some outside force that could be blamed for our own inability to accept silence.

I do not think there is such a thing as writer's block. There is merely a time to speak and a time to be silent. There is an in-breath and an out-breath. There is a time to absorb and a time to give away. There is conception, and gestation, and a time of birth. Certainly there are blocks in our lives, conditions that can stop the flow of our creativity, the flow of words. But I think what is commonly called writer's block is a symptom of a life-style where one constantly needs to show a product in order to be validated. As if a writer's business were only to write, and not to listen, to be, to sway silently in the movement of something yet unformed, the rhythm of the universe that is in us all the time.

When one goes for a walk, there is a rhythm, a certain movement with different phases to it. First one foot goes out, then the other. Certain stretches of the path are easier than others. For some people uphill is difficult, for some people downhill is difficult. It helps to pay attention to that. Our breathing changes. Sometimes it is fast and urgent, sometimes it is relaxed and calm. Our thought patterns change and our emotions, depending on where we are on the path. It helps to notice that too. I like to pay attention to the exact physical place where I am, and the feelings and thoughts I have as I move through those places. Perhaps I am walking through a large open meadow and a feeling of elation goes through me, perhaps an image comes into my mind at that time, and I try to remember it. I don't try to analyze it, I just pay attention that it came in that place, that it came when I walked calmly. Or perhaps the opposite happens. Maybe I am on a stretch of the walk where there is great intensity, perhaps I am crossing a city street between cars, perhaps I reach the other side and feel anxious, maybe the street is ugly and full of garbage, and I feel irritated.

Whatever it is, it is part of the walk, and to each part there is a certain movement. Perhaps I am walking with a friend, and there are certain times on that walk when I don't feel like talking at all. Sometimes we may both walk in complete silence and yet feel very much in tune with each other. Sometimes I may feel a great need to express, to point out something, to voice what I feel on the walk. All this is part of the movement of the walk also. There is a rhythm to it, there are phases to it—the silence, the talking, the joy, the irritation, the fast movement, and the calm movement, the in-breath, the out-breath, the expansion and the contraction—they are all part of the walk. They are all different movements, but they are all phases of one larger movement, the walk.

When it comes to writing, very similar things happen. And in our daily lives similar movements happen. That is why it is good to have a journal. It trains us to be aware of that. We can learn to respect each moment we are in, and to listen to it. If I am in a moment of great irritation, it helps me to recognize that. It may not feel good to be in such a state of irritation, but it is helpful to recognize that it is part of the path I am on, and to live through it with that awareness. And when it comes to writing in a journal, it is helpful to use that irritation for writing. Not to avoid it, or to falsify it into something else, but to use the energy of the difficult part of the path, to write. And at another time, use the energy of the calm, use the great elation you feel, for writing. Use each movement of life for what it is, and write in the journal from the recognition of that movement. Each will produce different types of writing. Certain movements of life produce no writing at all. What is called writer's block is often a refusal to recognize this.

It is all right not to write for a while. There are times in my life when I don't want to show my writing to anyone, not one single line. I don't want to read it, I don't want to send it out for publication, I don't even want to discuss it. And sometimes in fact I am not writing. But when that happens I pay attention to where my energy is, what phase I am in, what rhythm the universe has sent me. And I try to respect the situation I am in, as something that is right for now— perhaps it is time to make a new garden, or a new relation- ship, or a new house. Perhaps it is time to learn a new language, new images may surface which I do not yet understand, a new way of seeing may grow in me, and it is not time to form it yet. Maybe it is time to grieve for something, to rest in a state of silence, of unformed words, to walk on that part of the path. Maybe it is right to wait, to be receptive towards what new may come, but not to push it into form out of some impatience.

When it comes to my private journal, there are actually few times when I don't write at all. When I first began journal writing, there were often long stretches when I felt I could not write. But I began to recognize that those were the places in my life which I refused to talk about—I was afraid, and ashamed to write about them. As the years went by, I realized how much the writing actually helped me to get through these moments, how the journal made me conscious of the state I was in, how it helped me to accept the difficult times as passages. I began to move through them with greater ease, accepting both the passages through light and through dark. I also became aware that there was rarely a passage of pure darkness, that each difficult life experience can also have gifts and moments of joy. And one need only keep a detailed record of an entire day in one's ordinary life to see that such days are neither all light nor all dark. Such a day contains, on a small scale again, all the phases of our life rhythm, all the phases of the path. We fluctuate and vibrate, along with the rest of the pulsating universe, from cycle to cycle, from in-breath to out-breath, from expansion to contraction, from death to life. And the true calmness comes from recognizing this, and accepting it—that there are such cycles, in each hour, each day, each phase of our life. I use my journal to keep me conscious of that, and therefore there are very few times when I don't write at all. I may write very little, small notes, a dream recorded, tiny signals to myself, to recall later where I have been. Sometimes, during a time of silence, I write nothing at all. But now it is no longer a refusal to speak, rather it is a quiet waiting until the words begin to form again, until the cycle of silence moves into speech, all on its own.

EVENING

As soon as I had finished this morning's writing I went for a walk. It was my first walk in the city after my recent wilderness journey. The streets were crowded with Sunday walkers, and Sunday drivers, tourist buses, and families heading for a picnic in the park. As soon as I entered the park I felt a sense of irritation about all the people. I wanted the park to myself as a substitute for the wilderness I missed. Instead it was thriving with humans of every shape, color, and age. It wasn't until I saw a pink balloon waving at me from the top of a pine tree that I saw the humor in the situation, saw what sort of wilderness I was really entering and accepted the situation I was in. So I walked on and enjoyed myself in this man-made nature where thousands of humans simulated a day in the great outdoors, aided by cars and radios, picnic blankets, and baby strollers. After a while I found myself in front of the Academy of Sciences with its natural history museum inside. Then my sense of humor was truly delighted. I decided to walk in and enjoy a full tour of simulated nature. Here was man's collection of animals, plants, rocks, the stars, and even of man himself. I decided to walk in and move through the cycles of the universe right there and then.

My favorite place in that museum is the African Hall where there is a large scene of a water hole, with stuffed animals of the African grasslands and life-size plants and trees. This water hole scene goes through the complete cycle of a day within about twenty minutes, thanks to the aid of colored lights and a sound tape. We visitors are allowed to experience the magnificence of an African dawn, full of bird sounds and lions' roars, the quiet heat of midday, the rosy evening with all the sounds returning, and the night, with monkey screams and more lions' roars and all kinds of eerie noises. I love to sit there and experience the movements of this day—how the rhythm changes with the light, when there is peace, when there is anxiety. Sometimes I sit there for several days, that is, the simulated days of twenty minutes each. It is a great place for writing if one wants to observe how the changes in a day, the light and the sound, affect one's emotions, one's own rhythm, and one's writing. But today I did not do any writing there, not on paper anyway. But I paid attention to the children, the many children who squealed and ran back and forth, and those who stood still listening to the animal sounds. And I noticed how those children, the loud and the quiet ones, were affected by this cycle of light and sound in front of them, how they hushed with the fading of the light, how they listened to the dark. And more than most adults in the hall, the children flowed with the rhythm of this African day.

I moved on, strolling through the museum without a plan. At one time I found myself in the wilderness of New Guinea. Then I was in a room that simulated the terror of a San Francisco earthquake. The whole floor was shaking, and people were standing in line to experience this. I hoped it would shake them into a sense of aliveness, and I walked on through the planetary system, the Milky Way. Finally I arrived in the Hall of Man. And there in the middle of that hall was an exact replica of the wooden house the Indians of northern California had lived in. I had seen this dwelling in this hall before, but this time it affected me in a new way. Here were the house, the tools, the baskets, the salmon drying—from the exact area of the wilderness where I had just been, the very river where the salmon had rushed upstream. And suddenly I was very tired of the museum, of all this simulation. Perhaps the wild river woman who had snatched my papers had been right after all—there was no translation, everyone had to go to the source himself to understand, to listen to the true rhythms of the earth.

Once, the old Indian man told me that his grandmother had been a fine basket weaver, what a shame it was that all these live baskets were now in museums. He told me how each basket carries a spirit in it, the spirit of the song that was woven into it, and that spirit stays alive for a long time. I bent over the glass cases of the museum, and I listened intensely, for the live song, but I could not hear it. And yet as I looked and looked at these baskets, their fine geometric patterns of dark and light, I thought: Perhaps this grandmother left some inscription after all, a faint journal without sound.

Today, as I turned on the radio, there was a man playing the drum. The rhythm caught my attention immediately, and as I listened to it I was very moved. It was a simple but consistent beat. I felt very at home in it, and I just wanted it to go on and on. After a while the drummer stopped, and there was a discussion between him and another person. "What do you do," asked that person "to achieve this beautiful constant rhythm?" And the drummer said, "Well, it's really quite easy, all you have to do is keep to the exact rhythm of your heart. You follow your heartbeat, and the voice of the drum will come alive."

One could say the same for writing. Follow your heartbeat and your voice as a writer will come alive. I mean this literally and metaphorically. I once gave my students an exercise: I asked them to establish a slow and deep breathing pattern and then told them to write in the rhythm of their breathing. This brought out a flood of unexpected texts, and many of the students were totally amazed at what they had written. I then asked them to repeat this exercise, to listen to their breathing, but also to their heartbeat, and to write from that listening. What most people experienced was that their breathing and their heartbeat became one, but not just that, their language became one with their breathing/heart rhythm. And some of the texts that came out of this were so surprising and so beautiful that people were moved to tears.

The voice of the writer had literally become one with the heartbeat. All I had done was make them aware of the basic life rhythm they carried in their bodies. And by literally submitting their language to their own physical life rhythm, they had suddenly also experienced what that means metaphorically, and some of them understood for the first time what it means to have a voice.

One doesn't have to write to one's physical heartbeat in order to find one's voice as a writer. But it helps to know that language has to do with the breath, and that consciousness has to do with the heart. And by "knowing" I mean knowing this in one's body, the very body that has lungs and vocal cords and a mouth that forms words, this body out of which comes sound. This is my drum, I am the drum, and there is no other drum like me. And I have to learn what this drum sounds like, what is its deep voice, and how to bring it alive.

Many students have no idea what their voice is. They will admire someone else's voice—a well-known writer perhaps or a fellow student in class. They will say, "If only I could write like that." But I do not encourage them to learn by imitation. I encourage them to listen to their own voice: What is it that talks in you? What is it that wants to come out of you? I encourage them to listen with great attention to those other voices in class, to listen to those other heartbeats, until they can tell them apart—each person, each writer with his/her very own voice. Each voice like a fingerprint. Each drum with a sound and a pattern of its own, bringing forth its own story, its own song, its own life rhythm.

To listen to your voice in the literal sense is to become aware of the knowledge of the body, what pain and what joy is stored there, and how it affects the sound that comes out of your throat. Most people are terrified of reading their texts aloud in class. Yet I ask each person to do this. It is the fastest way to hear the voice in your body and to know if it is true to yourself.

To listen to your voice in the metaphorical sense is to know if you are falsifying yourself. It is to know if you are truly speaking from that deep inner need, the need which moves from your life and its very own rhythm, and which does not try to please an authority.

The voice that listens to its own heartbeat often sounds deceptively simple. But it takes courage to speak this way, to simply say, "This is what comes out of me, this is what wants to speak." Sometimes what wants to speak seems dark and terrifying, seems stupid, makes no sense. Then one needs to have the courage to let it sit there on the page for a while, to not destroy it, to look at it much later and to listen for one's voice in it. And often we realize in this way that the most beautiful part of us comes with a dark mask. Then we need to listen for the heartbeat, for that clear voice of the drum, to recognize ourselves.

As I look through pages and pages of my journal that I wrote over the years, I see it is a constant search for the clear voice of the drum. Sometimes false voices show up, voices that want to sound good, for posterity, or to fool myself, voices that are too cute, too pretentious, too eager to explain it all. But again and again there is this clear heartbeat, often just for a few moments, then again for pages. Often it comes disguised in ugly masks, things that were terrifying to say, but that after some time on the page lost their terror. When I read these pages after months or years, sometimes the finest voice comes out of them, and I want to cry for so frightening myself that I couldn't hear my own heartbeat through the dark mask, until years later. I want to cry for that deep voice that keeps singing and singing to us on our path, and we don't recognize it as our own.

SAN FRANCISCO
JULY 12
TUESDAY, MORNING

Yesterday I began to clear out the back room—boxes of books, dusty stuff. It's actually the nicest room in this large flat, but it is tiny. It looks out toward the ocean, and I have used it mostly for my sunset meditations. There is an old overstuffed chair facing the window, and I come here to sit at the end of the day, to send the sun around the world.

It is time for this room to have a new life. My niece will be arriving in another week to spend the summer with me, and I thought I would fix things up a bit. Her mother called from Europe to say that everything had been arranged and that the airlines would take care of the child. I was a little concerned about a thirteen-year-old traveling that far by herself, but Miss Adventuresome got on the phone herself and said she was excited.

So I started fixing up the room and got excited myself. But first I worried. What will this young girl do in all the hours that her strange aunt is writing? Well, I went and bought her a beautiful journal with a shiny painted cover and lots of lovely white pages. And colored markers for writing. Perhaps she would be enticed into this craft.

But when the room was cleaned out of all the old stuff, I had a new thought. Perhaps it wasn't the room that needed to be fixed, perhaps it was time for me to have a new life. To be a child, to play. To stop writing for a while and go on a wild adventure. I will take her into the wilderness. We will go on a magic journey together, touch the sacred places of the earth, swim in the live river.

And on second thought: Maybe we will write a travel journal together. Maybe not.

SAN FRANCISCO
JULY 14
THURSDAY, 2 P.M.

Whenever I come to the end of one of my journal notebooks, I feel a bit anxious and sad. I don't want to let go. Of what? I am not quite sure. It is easy to buy a new notebook and simply continue. But somehow each notebook has a life of its own, and perhaps what I don't want to let go of is the life lived in those pages. As soon as I get close to the end, I feel somehow that I have to bring to a conclusion all the big questions that came up in those pages, the development I went through during the last few months. My writing often intensifies, and I want to pour out on the last page some great insight that would help me transform. As if the new notebook were a new slate and I wanted to arrive there newly born, with my butterfly wings freshly opened, silky and without scar.

In truth, however, the end of a notebook rarely marks the end of a particular life process, but what it does mark sometimes is a shift in consciousness. Sometimes I take the new journal and I write a line on the inside cover, a line from a poem, a theme, something that I came across in my own previous writing, or in some other place, something that reminds me of the focus I would like to maintain for a while. This is how this book came about, this book about journal writing. There was a sentence I had underlined in my previous journal and it caught my attention when I reread it. It said, "The journal is a writing meditation, a walking meditation, a mystical journey." And as soon as I took that sentence out and focused on it, a new kind of notebook began to grow. I began to write this quest, began to live this process.

My sense is that this book is coming to an end, not because I am running out of pages or of things to say, but because I have gone for a certain walk, and the focus has completed itself. It's like walking along a field of sunflowers, being in the presence of their dark and radiant faces, and then coming to the end of the field. One could of course keep walking around and around and extend the walk, but at a certain point it is better to move on, to let another notebook begin, a new quest in a new field.

There is a sense of sadness about this. I have never before written a journal for the public. There is a sense that I have not walked alone, that all the unknown readers out there have come with me on this writing quest. And this journal was written in their presence. And besides the readers, to whom this book is addressed, there are other beings that took part in this writing meditation: A small turtle that sits on my desk and is the guardian of my words. All my teachers— whether spirit, human, animal, or plant, and especially the rocks that carry the journal of the earth. There are my students who came with me, providing examples from their own learning process, and walking along with great enthusiasm and encouragement for my book. And finally there is my brother, whose tragic death tore into the middle of this writing process. But he walked with me and transferred a presence I cannot explain.

When one writes a journal in the company of all these beings, one is reluctant to leave and wants to hold on to the process. It is at this point that we come to the ancient ceremony of the giveaway: You give away, instead of holding on to, what is precious to you.

I have never given away one of my journals to the public. But I am sure this must be the last and most beautiful part of the walk.

One day
I walked on the mountain
and the flute song
went through me.
That's all.
I became the reed
and the wind went through
and I wrote it down
in my journal.

About the Author

B. Nina Holzer, Ph.D., grew up in Austria and now lives in the United States. She is a bilingual writer and educator, and a trained body therapist. She is on the creative writing faculty of Foothill College, Los Altos, California, and also leads workshops, writing quests, group retreats, and wilderness camps to facilitate personal and community healing.

OTHER BELL TOWER BOOKS

Books that nourish the soul, illuminate the mind,
and speak directly to the heart

Valeria Alfeyeva. **Pilgrimage to Dzhvari:** *A Woman's Journey of Spiritual Awakening.* Hardcover 0-517-59194-4 (1993).

David A. Cooper. **Silence, Simplicity, and Solitude:** *A Guide for Spiritual Retreat.* Hardcover 0-517-58620-7 (1992).

The Heart of Stillness: *The Elements of Spiritual Practice.* Hardcover 0-517-58621-5 (1992).

Entering the Sacred Mountain: *A Mystical Odyssey.* Hardcover 0-517-59653-9 (1994).

James G. Cowan. **Letters from a Wild State:** *Rediscovering Our True Relationship to Nature.* Hardcover 0-517-58770-X (1992).

Messengers of the Gods: *Tribal Elders Reveal the Ancient Wisdom of the Earth.* Softcover 0-517-88078-4 (1993).

Marc David. **Nourishing Wisdom:** *A Mind/Body Approach to Nutrition and Well-Being.* Hardcover 0-517-57636-8 (1991); Softcover 0-517-88129-2 (1994).

Kat Duff. **The Alchemy of Illness.** Softcover 0-517-88097-0 (1993).

Noela N. Evans. **Meditations for the Passages and Celebrations of Life:** *A Book of Vigils.* Hardcover 0-517-59341-6 (1994).

Greg Johanson and Ron Kurtz. **Grace Unfolding:** *Psychotherapy in the Spirit of the Tao-te ching.* Hardcover 0-517-58449-2 (1991); Softcover 0-517-88130-6 (1994).

Marcia and Jack Kelly. **Sanctuaries—The Northeast:** *A Guide to Lodgings in Monasteries, Abbeys, and Retreats of the United States.* Softcover 0-517-57727-5 (1991).

Sanctuaries—The West Coast and Southwest. Softcover 0-517-88007-5 (1993).

One Hundred Graces, eds. Hardcover 0-517-58567-7 (1992).

Barbara Lachman. **The Journal of Hildegard of Bingen.** Hardcover 0-517-59169-3 (1993).

Gunilla Norris. **Being Home:** *A Book of Meditations.* Hardcover 0-517-58159-0 (1991).

Becoming Bread: *Meditations on Loving and Transformation.* Hardcover 0-517-59168-5 (1993).

Sharing Silence: *Meditation Practice and Mindful Living.* Hardcover 0-517-59506-0 (1993).

Ram Dass and Mirabai Bush. **Compassion in Action:** *Setting Out on the Path of Service.* Softcover 0-517-57635-X (1992).

Richard Whelan, ed. **Self-Reliance:** *The Wisdom of Ralph Waldo Emerson as Inspiration for Daily Living.* Softcover 0-517-58512-X (1991).

Bell Tower books are for sale at your local bookstore,
or you may call 1-800-733-3000 to order with a credit card.